If We
Are
Brave

ALSO BY THEODORE R. JOHNSON

*When the Stars Begin to Fall: Overcoming Racism
and Renewing the Promise of America*

If We Are Brave

ESSAYS
FROM BLACK
AMERICANA

THEODORE R. JOHNSON

AMISTAD

An Imprint of HarperCollinsPublishers

HarperCollins books may be purchased for educational, business, or sales promotional use. For information, please email the Special Markets Department at SPsales@harpercollins.com.

FIRST EDITION

Designed by Nancy Singer

Library of Congress Cataloging-in-Publication Data has been applied for.

ISBN 978-0-06-334645-1

24 25 26 27 28 LBC 5 4 3 2 1

In loving memory of my mother, Sandra Lee Johnson, and grandmother, Orrie Bell Lee—for gifting the passion and capacity to learn hard things, and for being my first readers.

Contents

Live from the Repast

I am a Gen X son of the Black South. I spent my childhood summers in Blakely, Georgia, with my grandparents and the steady stream of aunts and uncles and cousins who traveled from points up north for weeklong stays. My favorite memories of those days are the times when everyone was home, usually around the Fourth of July. There was food in every inch of the kitchen. Meat on the grill. The eatin' was always good.

And then, without fail, the time came when these all-day cookouts splintered into after-dinner salons and rap sessions, always gendered. The men outside. The women inside or on the porch. Everyone is full. The glassy eyes say some are sleepy after waking at the crack of dawn and that others have had as much to drink as to eat. Children's laughter and running are everywhere—switches for smart mouths, too. In these country summers with lightning bugs blinking around men's bravado and tobacco, the laughing and philosophizing begin. No long story is ever made short out here. Some of the shorter stories are tales, completely made up. The men are in a semicircle, either around the grill with ashy charcoal sheltering a red ball of heat, or gathered around a fryer, dropping the last bit of catfish that'll be at breakfast tomorrow. There are dogs lying around, eyes begging, and the roads are dirt.

The women have their own thing. Stories bounce around on the laughs, the *kee-kee*ing. We can hear their voices in the night but cannot make out the words. When I wander inside, I'm hurried away. "Go back outside," they say. The part always left unsaid is *with the men*. So I go, grabbing pound cake on the way out.

Back with the uncles and grown cousins, I pull up a chair but stay out of the way. The night's wisdom only comes when the children are invisible. The stories. The rhythm. The turning over of news and ideas, examining them for truth. The baritone chuckles of old men saying the most ridiculous things, a cigarette in one hand and a beer or mason jar in the other. "If I tell you a duck could pull a truck, shut up and hook the sucker up!"

I learn out here while my sisters and the nieces get their schooling from the ladies' caucus. Inside and out, the life lessons are invaluable. The way to connect. The way to tell a story. The way to share. What to share. We young folk don't know that it's happening, but we are being molded, shaped by a culture older than everything around us. Country Black philosophizing exceeds Plato's in my world, where the elders' insights are far sharper than those of the people the world believes to be better.

The mark of adulthood in these scenes is when you're no longer invisible. Outside, it is a rite of passage for a young man to be invited into the conversation, to be given the floor. Some squander the moment, jumping in before they're ready. It isn't pretty. The humbling that occurs in these rituals is not for the meek. Others seize it and soar. A few are pulled off the sidelines, whether they like or not, because it was time. After I went off to fancy schools and the military, my reentry into these circles came with questions about all things politics, race, war, and so on.

Tell me something, nephew . . . is a siren song. It's an invitation to ruin as much as a chance to shine. Will playful embarrassment follow? Or maybe I'll win the day, making the old men laugh so hard, drinks are spit out and coughing fits sound from all directions. Here *He a fool!* is a compliment. But no matter one's education or profession, the younger conversationalists are reminded there are smarts and kinds of intelligence that universities and institutions cannot teach, that other worlds either do not value or do not understand. When these circles are at their best, you learn who your people are. Where you come from. Where you fit in. That you belong. If you can hold your own here, you can hold it anywhere, with any kind of people.

I am writing in the pages that follow like I am trying to explain my views on things in the storytelling ways of those wise souls on dark summer nights around charcoal embers, swatting at mosquitos and flies. Sometimes my life gets in the way—I am a product of the military and churches and universities and being a Black boy in the white suburbs and the South and other places. It's impossible to miss. It's in the approach, the language, the timbre. But I am also the kin of countryfolk gathered together, just rapping on the Fourth of July. It's all here, trying to say something smart without being smart-mouthed about it.

Some of it might strike your ear oddly. Some of it will rankle. It is supposed to. It's about race and democracy in the United States—it can't help but be uncomfortable.

Ultimately, I mean to say something of substance in an interesting way. When it's about a thing that I know that I know, it lands on the page structured and formalistic in the way that the outside world expects learning to be demonstrated. When it's about a thing that I think that I think, the ideas sort of meander and tumble out. I'm freestyling. Philosophizing. Hoping to land on the point I've been trying to make all night. It's a cipher. And whether it comes out like a professor writing in a newspaper or something more casual and cultural, the ways of those summer nights are always the guide.

The invisible character in every story is the telling of it, in how it's told.

• • •

At sixteen, I bought a cassette that contained one of the most famous rap debuts ever. Main Source was the group's name, and the song was "Live at the Barbeque." The rapper Nas, now one of the greats, introduced himself to the world in that song, stringing together metaphors about religion and race and other things that just weren't said in the world where I grew up. *Before steppin' to me, you'd rather step to Jehovah.* It was too much. I listened to it on repeat until it wasn't.

The title of the song is perfect. It feels like a bunch of young dudes sitting in a semicircle at a cookout, philosophizing about life. Bragging and lying and telling hard truths. In a way, Queens, New York, could be Blakely, Georgia. It is summer and hot, and there's food. The men gather to talk in one place. The women another. The kids play. And we hear ideas and stories and emotions that teach us, stretching and testing us. These salons and rap sessions are everywhere. Barbershops. Sorority meetings. Stoops. Dorm rooms. But when they are in churches, in the solemn or respectable moments, the character changes. These are repasts. They're held at houses of worship following something routine like First Sunday service or something previously unimaginable, like the death of a loved one.

These places and moments are touchier. The situations more delicate. But the ritual is still performed. The men find their way outside to the parking lot. The women inside, gathered and off-limits to me, except when beckoned to move this thing or bring that. Hard conversations are still had. Repasts sometimes host the hardest conversations we will ever have. We must be more delicate there. But no less honest.

This is what I mean to do. To come Live from the Repast.

CHAPTER I

American Heathen

Altar call at the Black church of my youth was serious business. I am sure it is meaningful in lots of ways in lots of other places, but for those churches—where ushers are white-gloved sentries at the sanctuary doors, where deaconesses drape cloths over midiskirted women who've fallen to the floor after rubbing elbows with the Holy Spirit, and where church fans with hip dips and Black history icons are steadily waving to cool the temples of those on fire for the Lord—altar call is the spiritual culmination of the Sunday service. It is the place and time where people seeking special prayer move to the front of the church, taking a public step toward the will and mercy of God, hoping to get a taste of grace. They go to lay their troubles down—to seek relief or guidance or an extra helping of faith. There is crying. Some folks holler. Others are calm, hushed, quietly meditating. Anxious energy routinely crescendos to a fever pitch, a sanctified electricity pulsing in the air and coursing through the mass of bodies gathered for altar call and the ones filling the pews. And at my Raleigh, North Carolina, childhood church, performative displays of worship were part of the weekly ritual—the urgent, tight-stepped praise-dancing of those who caught the ghost, and the speaking in stuttered tongues with punching enunciations coming from those consumed by it. Listen, this part of the Black church can be theatric, but believers do not play.

It is into this solemn and chaotic experience that I entered as a teen on one otherwise nondescript Sunday afternoon many years ago. My nerves were on edge, my face dialed to serious. I felt a sudden urge to be prayed over by the pastor, who was surrounded by a makeshift oval of hopefuls awaiting his attention and hands of anointing, his fingers glistening with olive oil, painting miniature crosses on their foreheads. I cautiously made my way across the plush royal-red carpet leading to the front of the church—avoiding Sister So-and-So staggering to and fro, watching out for Brother Such-and-Such's swinging arms keeping beat with his rhythmic *Hallelujah*s. I do not remember feeling troubled about anything in particular—no recollection of any pressing family issues or worries over tests and grades or stressing over unrequited puppy love for a girl who couldn't care less. I was just an uncertain and insecure teenager looking for some certainty and security.

The encounter with the pastor came and went without incident. He stepped in front of me, put the palm of his right hand on my forehead and his left hand on my shoulder, and began, "Lord, we pray that you bless Teddy . . ." I mostly zoned out, feeling no ghost, no revelation or rush of anything rapturous. But then, the prayer completed and his hands braced on my arms, he looked me dead in the eyes to say eight words that I will never forget and to which I may ascribe deeper meaning than may be due: "God has a special plan for your life."

Maybe he said those words to everyone, a sort of punctuation to the prayer, like a flattering *Amen* disguised as personal prophecy. Perhaps it was not a message straight from the good Lord above meant just for me in that moment, but that is how I took it. I believed it.

I cannot say this strongly enough—*I believed it.*

I am sure my eyes got a little wide, my face—still rounded with youth—shocked to stillness. And more than three decades later, with age and wisdom and skepticism now wrinkled into my forehead and filling the puffs under my eyes, I still believe it. No clue what it means; no idea what this special plan is supposed to be. But in the grand scheme of things, the *what* of it all is immaterial, it makes no difference. The thing that mattered most then, as now, is the sense of purpose it gave me. It told me that I was here on this earth to do something only I could do. It said, "Relax. God got you." It was Providence.

PROVIDENCE. I USE THIS WORD on purpose. It has an important feel to it, like an invocation of something. I do not remember my first encounter with it, but when I hear it now, oddly enough, it reminds me of high school US history class.

The men who dreamed up the United States could not keep that word off their tongues or out of the ink in their quills. And their gaslighting was thorough. John Jay sweet-talked the new nation with the word, telling a particular kind of white lie in suggesting that "this country and this people seem to have been made for each other, and it appears as if it was the design of Providence."[1] The closing of the Declaration of Independence reads, "With a firm reliance on the protection of divine Providence, we mutually pledge to each other our Lives, our Fortunes and our sacred Honor."[2] Benjamin Franklin made the case that the creation of the United States was only due to the "frequent instances of a superintending Providence in our favor."[3] George Washington wrote that we can "trace the finger of Providence"[4] to our democracy established by the ratification of the Constitution. The nation's creation, solidarity (exaggerated as it was), and democracy are all owed to Providence, to let the founders tell it.

All this talk about our country's Providence, however, should not be too reassuring, because I am told on good authority that American democracy is presently headed to hell in a handbasket. And if I learned nothing else in the Baptist church, the one thing you do not want to be is on the way to hell.

Given the state of our system of government, the concern is understandable. It is painfully clear that too many of our elected leaders do not adhere to any principle except demonize thy neighbor. The folks who are supposed to be the caretakers of our democracy seem more interested in becoming political celebrities than governing. They turn everything into an argument and then deliberately blow it out of proportion, making mountains out of molehills just so they can push half of the country down the side. Economic inequality is off the charts, and race relations remain a national flash point. Democratic systems are fraying; our institutions, eroding. There are all kinds of dirty money and disinformation floating around in our politics and elections. Our congressional districts are gerrymandered. States across the country are laying legislative land mines between the ballot box and voters, hoping to amputate the voices of folks deemed undesirable. And, to top it all off, it feels like Americans are increasingly more openly intolerant of one another. It's a mess.

I can't help but wonder, though, if this truly signals a system on the cusp of collapse, or if these are just the latest signs of what American democracy has always been: a thing never intended for use by its namesake—the *dêmos*, or the people. Rather, it was originally designed for a very select few who, we have been told, know better than the rest of us. So, when the United States enslaved Black Americans, the nation said it was practicing democracy. When it denied women the vote, dispossessed Native Americans of land, and oppressed new arrivals from Europe to Asia, it called itself a democracy. When campaigns of racist terrorism ripped through the country during Jim Crow, depriving Black people of their constitutional rights to equal protection under the law and freedom from discrimination at the voting booth? Democracy. Having democracy here at home, however, was not enough; the country also wanted to export it. When the United States initiated its foray into the First World War, its declared national purpose was to make the rest of the world "safe for democracy"—even though *democracy* was kicking the ass of a great many of us here at home.

Today folks of all races and ethnicities and in every region of the country are wondering to themselves and aloud, *Where is the democracy that's supposed to deliver equality and opportunity? 'Cause this ain't it.* When the people who've been left out hear the alarming news that democracy is on its way to hell, you will need to excuse them for greeting the bulletin with a tender chuckle and a pitying *Bless your heart.* They wonder how on earth other folks didn't know the version of democracy that they've been getting went to hell long ago.

And yet it is largely a foregone conclusion—even among those in groups who have suffered the most—that a government working for the people is a sacred system that must be pursued and preserved. You can put me in that number, too. But I also think we would be doing ourselves a disservice if we did not, on occasion, question the unquestionable. It borders on sacrilege, perhaps—the province of heathens and faithless provocateurs—but it must be asked and answered to satisfaction: What's so special about America and its democracy?

• • •

ONCE, WHEN I WAS TWELVE or maybe thirteen years old, I asked the elder brother leading Bible study why it was that God sent a commandment that said *Thou shalt not kill*, but then helped David slingshot a rock through Goliath's dome. Initially, he had a blank deer-in-headlights look that lasted a couple uncomfortable heartbeats. Behind his darting eyes, I could see the gears grinding, working to find an answer. And then he said some words, none of which satisfied my genuine curiosity about this seemingly hypocritical behavior from the heavens. In the end, the gist of the answer was basically the well-traveled response that cannot be debated, the one deployed whenever things do not seem to add up: *The Lord works in mysterious ways.* Well, yes. Biblical tales of immaculate conceptions, talking donkeys, and folks turning into pillars of salt or getting swallowed by whales or trying to build a skyscraper to heaven or loitering in a lion's den without becoming the repast are certainly some odd ways of doing business. But the elder brother's answer sufficed. It had to. In my church, the thing second to not questioning the Lord is the unspoken gospel of not questioning grown folks.

But then, several years after the pastor's special-plan ordination during altar call, I came across a book titled *A History of God.* It was written by Karen Armstrong, an Irish woman who was a nun in the Society of the Holy Child Jesus within the Roman Catholic church before rethinking her religion and becoming a writer and scholar on it. Her lived experience, stitching together total devotion to a religious order and deep research that questioned everything about it, provided a perspective on religion that was catnip to my increasingly curious mind. The first words of the first chapter changed my world. They ran so counter to everything I had been taught that it felt almost blasphemous to read. "In the beginning," Armstrong starts, echoing the opening of the Bible before turning to this disruption, "human beings created a God who was the First Cause of all things and Ruler of heaven and earth."[5] I could hardly believe my eyes: Human beings *created* a God?? Lawd Jesus.

The book goes on to discuss Christianity, Islam,

Judaism, and other religions, revealing their similarities, differences, and intersections. She details contradictions and intriguing little insights, like how Genesis appears to have two different creation stories in its first two chapters. But the book generally suggests that the idea of God evolves as people do and, as a result, that God has two choices: either keep up with us, the people, or get replaced.

Leaving aside the arguments for and against Armstrong's analysis of God and religion, the framing of the issue in this way was enlightening. Thinking of the divine and the sacred as an idea of human origin forced me to tackle the first principles of my faith and ask exactly whose idea of God I had adopted and why. If I could not answer these questions, then Providence and "special plans" were meaningless. So the only way forward on this—and anything like it—was to give myself permission to challenge that which I was taught was unchallengeable.

IN THE UNITED STATES, DEMOCRACY is such an unchallengeable thing—sacred and self-evident.

This makes me a heathen.

Not because I do not believe but because I want to be convinced.

Democracy is more than just a system of government. To speak of American democracy is to comment on the nation's identity, history, character, and customs. When most people say *democracy*, they are not talking about institutions and processes and power arrangements; they are referring to a culture filled with an implicit knowledge of how things are supposed to be: that people are equal and should be treated fairly . . . that our voice matters and should be respected . . . that government works for the people and should not be an undue burden without a just cause. They have an idea of what the world should look like, and democracy is the tool that shapes it. And so, in various ways, we have come to believe American democracy is inherently good because it symbolizes and is intimately connected to us as a people, and to our own desires for the country. Then, like the cross for a not-insignificant number of Christians or the gun to Second Amendment zealots or the flag to intolerant nationalists, the symbol becomes more sacred than the values it's supposed to represent—love thy neighbor, self-defense, inclusive solidarity.

In the same way that people have used religion to justify doing evil, when America's democracy is all symbol and no principle, undertaking antidemocratic actions in its name is easily justified. A deep reverence soon emerges for a hollow, lip-serviced idea of democracy. And you'd better not be too critical of it; those who have disputed the sanctity of American democracy or pointed to its hypocrisy and shortfalls have often been declared unpatriotic at best and enemies of the state at worst. To be American and have an avowed love for something other than our democracy is a special kind of treason, the kind that makes one a civic sinner, a black sheep. This is worse than being a nonbeliever; this is enemy territory.

The problem is that many of us do not share a common vision for a democratic system in action and, worse, don't share a common vision for the United States. This all means it can be—it *has been*—dangerous to blindly accept that our democracy is the pinnacle of achievement in human governance. It leaves space neither for critique nor for us to develop an appreciation for it by arriving to that conclusion on our own. It means that when all the paradoxes show up—democracy being comfortable coexisting with slavery and oppression and dispossession and state violence—well, that is just democracy working in mysterious ways. True devotion to someone or something, however, emerges and deepens when it's earned, not when it's forced. The only way the earning is possible is if we give ourselves permission to question whether the thing is worth our trust and our faith and our energies. And as we identify where it falls short, it must not be considered so providential that it cannot be reshaped and touched up; rather, it should be updated, subjected to our fiddling to force its improvement.

In moments like these, we have a choice. The unpleasant one is to dig up our beliefs, shake the dirt and excess off the root, and examine what remains. The less disruptive option is to simply *Have faith, child* and let the Moving

Hand make the thing be whatever it will. As restrictive as this latter kind of thinking can be, there is an odd comfort in being anchored in something that is unwavering. It provides a compass by which to orient our actions and a scale by which to gauge them. Whether something is verifiably true is sometimes less important to us than whether it is constant, steady, reliable . . . that it does not disrupt too much. It's an imperfect way to live—grounding ourselves to an unchanging something can hinder our ability to grow and mature; grounding to something harmful can destroy us. But in a world where information and influences are swirling about us and ever changing, a baseline truth offers a rock where we can inscribe an enduring sense of ourselves and our identity. The allure of it is not that the thing is true but that it is fixed and solid and predictable. And this can be desirable for the human condition because our emotional and psychological well-being is meaningfully connected to the safety found in familiarity and stability.

The folks who study this say a stable identity helps avoid anxieties about our purpose and existence, and so we can avoid having to question every single thing that is around us and happening to us.[6] In other words, we have a story we tell ourselves about ourselves that gives us meaning and a filter for engaging with the world. And that meaning can be interrupted when the core elements of our identity and lives—stories, experiences, histories, relationships, routines, institutions, worldviews—are threatened. When someone bumps the table and makes our record skip or rips some pages out of our novella, an identity crisis can ensue.

• • •

WHEN THE PREACHER TOLD ME that God had a special plan for my life, I immediately anchored myself to that declaration. Each experience and relationship after that served a greater purpose. We have all heard the phrase that is intended to comfort when we cannot make sense of the world around us: *Everything happens for a reason.* The problem, of course, is that no one tells us what the reason is. For me, for a while, I didn't have to wonder—I was covered by a divine plan; that was reason enough. The stability of my conviction helped me weather whatever life hurled my way. And I was not alone in leaning on this rock—I cannot seem to spend a single day on social media without a member of my Black Southern peoples sharing this Scripture from Jeremiah: *"For I know the plans I have for you,"* declares the Lord, *"plans to prosper you and not to harm you, plans to give you hope and a future."*[7] And if that one does not get you together, Romans is often not far behind: *And we know that all things work together for good to them that love the Lord, to them who are the called according to his purpose.*[8] That's Providence straight, no chaser.

Americans, generally, have a sense of a special plan, of national Providence and destiny. Many have mostly bought into the consecration of our country and our democracy lock, stock, and barrel—sometimes, literally. It grounds us, directs us. Our beacon *should* be the Promise of America— that we are all created equal, that we have inalienable rights, that government derives its just powers from the consent of the governed. Instead, we have elevated a superficial and commercial conception of democracy to be our North Star. Being in the pews of democracy means that when it is used to violate the ideals of equality or solidarity, we are told it is done in service of a higher calling and that some rights for some people might need to be withheld, or put on hold. Just as folks have long used religion as a vehicle for violence and persecution, so, too, has democracy been weaponized to accomplish undemocratic things. Facing that ugly truth is its own kind of hell—it's easier to believe that America and democracy are inherently good, accept that sometimes bad people use them for bad reasons, and then return to the haven that reassures us Providence has the matter handled, explaining away our shortcomings by reasserting that everything happens for a reason.

As comforting as the certitude of democracy's goodness may be, exercising the unpleasant option of critically examining our beliefs is the way we learn if we actually want the democracy we have and whether we truly understand what it is—not the textbook definition of it but what it becomes when Americans pull the thing off the page and affix it to a country. Questioning democracy is the only way we can know what the first principles of American democracy are and how it is shaped by the nation's identity, history, and culture. And only once we have a clear view of these things can we answer the question: *What makes American democracy so special?* But we have to make the journey to discover the answer instead of allowing some old-fashioned indoctrination to drop us off at the point of conviction.

And so, here in this handbasket to hell, we should ask what precisely we mean when we invoke Providence in America. If our nation is the last best hope of the earth, as Abraham Lincoln once proclaimed, either the children can have faith, or they can take the more difficult path and interrogate the consecration. If we are brave, we are likely to find that most of us have not given much deep thought to what Americanism is or what is meant by the word *democracy*—though we are quick to employ the latter as a symbolic confession of our faith in the American experiment, strewn about our conversations like patriotic confetti. And then, if pressed to put words to what we think and feel about how America should work, we will find that ours do not match those of others given the same question. We all can see it, but our minds create vastly different versions.

While we are busy screaming that the country and democracy need saving, it would be helpful to know if we understand those words the same way, if we are fighting for the same ideals. I don't think we are. Some of us believe the democracy of previous generations was a purer form from which the country has strayed; many of us believe our democracy to have always been corrupt and incessantly oppressive, and want to reimagine it for the present and posterity. For some, equality and democracy mean a capitalistic meritocracy wherein the cream rises to the top, and those at the height of politics, the economy, and culture are there because of their talents and deft navigation of institutions. Others view equality and democracy as obligations to each other such that no one bunch of us gets either too far behind or too far ahead.

If you take a person from each of these groups and ask, *Do you believe in equality? Do you believe in democracy? Justice? Liberty?*, they'll answer with an enthusiastic yes. And, upon seeing agreement, they'll jump up from the table to get to work, only to notice they have charged off in different directions to accomplish very different things. Calls for unity or to "save democracy" rarely result in either because we are often working at cross-purposes, cloaked in appeals to values we're supposed to share. It is quite hard for a diverse people to work together to save a thing when they cannot agree on what the thing is. And nothing reveals this reality with such stark clarity as the way the most persistent and severe racial inequalities have shaped the nation.

Before we determine the direction and destination of this country, we must get it firmly in hand. And that is only possible if we interrogate what happens when we, the *dêmos*, bump against one another on the issues, norms, and cultures that shape the American way of life. This jostling is its own kind of democratic deliberation, a questioning and testing of our faith. It's the only way to truly decipher who and what America will be, come hell or high water.

• • •

A FEW YEARS AGO, THE woman who gave me life passed away in the evening hours following Mother's Day. For two decades, she'd beaten cancer each time it had appeared. She was a walking miracle, an answered prayer. But the fourth battle proved to be the final one. Her death caused me to do the previously unthinkable: doubt the existence—and the utility—of God.

My mom was a special soul. Not because she was mine, but because of her compassion, concern, and care for others. She was so loving and selfless that I wouldn't have believed it possible if I hadn't seen it for myself. And in a world in desperate need of more people like her, she was taken too soon. Robbed from us. How could any benevolent God allow that to happen? And why believe in a callous or disinterested one that would permit it?

Those are big questions. My rearing in the Black church and by the American South taught that you don't question God and grown folk. But some things demand answers, and there was no one else to ask. Neither of them could help me make sense of any of it. In place of an explanation, there were mostly words meant to comfort and give purpose to tragedy: "The Lord works in mysterious ways." I lost patience with it all.

Something happens when the beliefs and ideas most fundamental to your worldview are challenged or fractured. The experience invites deep inquiry into identity and the proper order of things. We mature when we use these moments to take stock of ourselves. Questioning the previously unquestionable and challenging core convictions help separate what we believe from what we've been told and assumed to be true. Such introspection can give a certain clarity to the things happening around us and new ways to see the past.

For the first twenty years of my life, we were in church three times a week. It was more than just religion. It was a community, its own distinct society. Raised in the Southern suburbs of the 1980s, I found in church the only place other than my house where I wasn't in the minority. There was social and cultural education there, points of deep pride. Kids had responsibilities—in the choir, as ushers, or reading a morning passage. Praise dancing and church fans never stopped on Sunday afternoons. My mother was a musician and directed the choir. If you ask me what I believe, I will point to her at that piano, singing at morning service.

But once she was gone, I started to see proof of her

everywhere. Not only in my belief system and my lens for viewing a complicated world, but in the smaller things. Like the cardinal that arrives at the bird feeder the moment I look. She is in the aromas of my kitchen, and in the songs she used to sing or play. Increasingly, I see her in my face, my temperament, in how I say certain words. I talk to her often—my inner monologues nodding to her as though she's in the audience: "Ma, you won't believe this . . . "

I think she'd get a kick out of it. Seeing her firstborn sitting outside on hot days, like she did, with a cold tomato in one hand and a saltshaker in the other. Learning the ways and moments and places where those who love her still find her. Knowing that we see her in the sunsets, at the golden time of day, as she wanted. And in the rainbows, too, received as a mother's gentle encouragement to live well.

In my refusal to let go of her, a simpler faith emerged. There was no need for mythology. No desire to let grief have the last word or be the strongest memory. She was still around, just differently now. It has been a journey to get to this point, and, admittedly, I still have no answers to those big questions. Sometimes, there is no answer. Faith doesn't promise miracles and answered prayers; it only promises that they are possible. And they are. I know because my mother was both.

A few days before she passed, I stopped at the nurses' station outside her hospital room for an update. One of them stood slowly—reverently, it seemed—and gave a rundown of the previous night. The report was positive enough, but the nurse's eyes confirmed what my heart already knew.

Without thinking, I started singing her praises. I needed them to know she was special, and not just because she was mine. After going on for a bit, struggling to find the right words, I asked, "You know how, when someone dies, people only talk about the person's best qualities and best moments at the funeral and leave everything else out?"

They all nodded.

"Well, with my mother, there is nothing to leave out. Nothing. She is an angel on this earth."

MY MOTHER DID NOT CURSE. In all the years we had together, I never heard her say or saw her write or even mouth a curse word. Except once, on January 6, 2021, four months before her death.

On that day, a crazed throng of Americans who believed the presidential election had been stolen attacked the US Capitol intending to overturn the election, seriously injuring police officers and threatening to kill congressional members and the vice president along the way. The snarling faces and oversize Confederate flags and unruly anarchy billowing through the halls of Congress transformed into a veritable lynch mob, looking to subdue a struggling democracy with one end of rope around its neck and the other end flung taut over the marbled branches of government. The spectacle played out on television and social media before a stunned world.

At 3:08 p.m., my mother texted me, What the hell?? Childlike cursing to most of us, but not from her.

The surprise of seeing that word from her sat astride the shock from watching the previously unfathomable scenes of violence and chaos at the Capitol. Of all the stresses she'd encountered in life since my birth in the summer following her twenty-third birthday—marriage, raising children, work, money, church leadership, the loss of parents and siblings, discrimination based on her race and sex—the event that extracted a curse word from her pious heart was the blame slung at Black voters, blame that fed an assault on American democracy in the months before she passed.

Donald Trump clumsily crocheted a web of scandalous lies that was infuriating, accusing Black people in Atlanta, Philadelphia, Milwaukee, and Detroit of voter fraud. It was not lost on my mother that some Americans, many who couldn't stomach a Black president years earlier, opted to attempt a dismantling of democracy rather than accept an election outcome that would make Kamala Harris the first Black woman to be vice president. For my mother, a child raised in Jim Crow Georgia, the stew of words and symbols and anger and violence dripping from the Capitol rioters and their enablers was all too familiar. Her disappointment was thick with disgust at the actions of the riotous horde and layered with the embarrassment that sometimes comes with assuming America is better than this—and the reminder that some of us aren't.

If our democracy is being ushered into the abyss, January sixth was the day its arms and legs were gathered into the handbasket for the journey.

What the hell, indeed.

...

STAVING OFF THE END OF OUR DEMOCRACY requires that we reimagine America, just as I had to do to keep my mother present and locate a beneficent God. It requires that we create a new story and identity and culture—not from scratch, because our origin is too important to who we have become and who we will be, but a creation through the process of evolution. Like Armstrong's opening line about human beings creating a God, Americans are the blacksmiths of our nation.

Providence did not build this country; it did not send our founding ideals on stone tablets down from some divine mountain or demand on penalty of eternal damnation that people operate like some are more equal than others. This country is the product of its people, not the other way around. Providence is ours, dutiful and obedient. It is what we make it. Democracies. Republics. They are our creations. We can do with them whatever we so choose, be it for ill or for the good of us all.

Reimagination, however, is tricky business. It arises from the premise that who we are is no longer sufficient or is deeply flawed in some way. Ego—whether personal or national—does not like confronting that truth. It's uncomfortable and invites an identity crisis. When a nation as large and diverse as the United States is overdue for a reimagination, those at the center of the national narrative are likely to feel threatened. The call for a new America is sometimes misunderstood as a declaration that the predominant culture has outlived its usefulness and needs to be replaced. Sometimes it's interpreted as an accusation that the nation in its current form is deficient, fraudulent, and unworthy of our appreciation. Reimagining our country does not mean reshuffling racial groups in a hierarchy. It does not suggest that the ideals on which the nation was founded should be stricken and give way to some other set of values or principles. It does not claim that our nation's history is little more than a collection of oppression and holds no moments or people or cultures to be proud of. No, reimagination means taking a breath to assess where we have gotten away from our professed aspirations and correcting our course to arrive at a better version of ourselves. Growth, change—these things are not easy, but they are necessary and central to us as a people and to this American experiment.

If we fail to recreate our nation and its democracy for our time, we will declare ourselves the projects' pallbearers. A nation founded on an idea must maintain faith in it for it to persist—to lose faith is to cause the death of the idea, and for this country, the death of the idea is the death of the nation itself. The geopolitical entity known as the United States doesn't need ideals to survive; democracy, as history has shown, can find a way to live even when the people's participation is restricted and funneled through a ruling class disinterested in the well-being of the common person. But America, defined by the Promise and the idea that a diverse nation can become one people, cannot ride shotgun with a system that encourages and perpetuates inequality and injustice. Something's gotta give. If we do not keep it fresh and current for the world we live in, those who feel cut out from the national narrative will not stand idly by. Their exclusion will fuel conflict with the very people they must build a country with.

The moment we are in is not unprecedented. The nation has had to reimagine itself multiple times over the course of its nearly 250-year existence. Just decades after the nation's founding, its westward expansion forced an identity crisis grounded in a series of questions, including the expansion of slavery, an evolving economy, violence against Native American tribes and other countries, and the immigration of white Europeans. The Civil War was the ultimate reimagination of America, which occurred only after the blood of more than a million people was spilled, the Reconstruction Amendments constituting a veritable second founding. Jim Crow, women's suffrage, the Great

Depression and the New Deal, the Civil Rights Movement, the Cold War, the Global War on Terrorism—each of these, to varying degrees, compelled the country to rethink itself and make policy choices based on its conclusion about who it believed it should be. Sometimes that meant making tremendous progress toward the nation's professed ideals by extending citizenship and the benefits of our constitutional democracy to more people, and sometimes it meant taking regressive and protectionist positions that actively rolled back civil rights under the guide of security—or to protect an imagined exclusionary vision for the United States. The desire and propensity for change are part of the American DNA, but the direction and magnitude of that change have always been a source of conflict.

· · ·

THIS TIME WILL NOT BE DIFFERENT. And it will not be easier. But it remains no less necessary than it was in previous generations. The urgency for action hasn't changed.

This is where this book begins, before the point of conviction that asserts Providence has deemed our country and our democracy and any one group of us exceptional. This book steps away from that presumed gospel and into the place of uncertainty through which true believers must travel if their faith is to be a thing of substance and not of empty public performances. Instead of an analytical deconstruction of American democracy and the system that girds it, this book describes what it looks like when it's discussed, when it's practiced by people who learn along the way that their sense of it differs in significant ways from their friends, families, coworkers, neighbors, and the democratic strangers with whom they must share the country. It brings an inquisitive spirit to our everyday experiences in hopes that it will lay bare the actual first principle of our democracy: that it must emerge from a morally egalitarian, multiracial society—anything else is a cheap imitation of our treasured ideals.

This book takes on questions of American identity, explores how racial and ethnic minority groups negotiate equality and opportunity among one another, wonders whether the country is comfortable with a democracy run by the people brought here to be its footstool, and reframes issues like voting and policing to demonstrate they are flashing warning signs of the first principles problem we have in this country. It puts Americans in conversations with one another instead of in arguments about systems. It wages the idea that the essence of democracy's problems shows itself with stark clarity when we pay closer attention to the people in the system. If our democracy is going to hell, it's because we lack a culture of democracy that works to the benefit of the full *dêmos*.

At its core, this book deliberates. It meanders; life is

complicated. And it does this from the vantage point of one of the nation's darker brothers, stamped with a story.

We are in it—this handbasket, this new beginning. We're likely in the throes of a third founding, well underway. The *dêmos* will either create here the last best hope of the earth or do something altogether different and undeniably worse. Whatever the special plan is for this country, we will be its authors, olive oil glistening on the tips of our fingers.

CHAPTER 2

Democracy When Black,

Parts I & II

PART I: VOTERS

Well into my thirties, I tried something new. Voting. It's embarrassing to admit. I was raised better than that.

But I didn't feel too guilty. I was an officer in the US Navy and had deployed enough times to the Middle East to earn a little civic grace. That's preserving democracy, too. Besides, the blame's not all mine: when my eighteenth birthday arrived, the government met the milestone with a postcard requiring registration for the military's draft. There was no such insistence on voter registration, a subtle suggestion that it's less important. And so, by the time Barack Obama won the Democratic primary, I was a military guy who'd spent many months on the ocean and not a second in a voting booth.

This apathy does not run in the blood. My parents were products of the Civil Rights era and the Jim Crow South and, as such, religiously exercised the hard-won right to vote. In my formative years, the house's politics pressed together progressive demands for racial equality with the Black conservatism of marathon church services that stretch deep into Southern Sunday afternoons. My parents and I differed in degree on any number of issues, but elections are where our politics really diverged. Like most Black folk, my mother was a lifelong Democrat, staying true even as the party vacillated in and out of her good graces. Before Donald Trump, my father was a somewhat perfunctory Republican—an heirloom from Black Americans' early-twentieth-century preference for the party of Lincoln, stamped in the familial name carried by my grandfather, father, and me: Theodore Roosevelt Johnson. And found in its libertarian strain that runs through Black Power's message of self-determination and economic self-sufficiency—a movement that influenced my dad in his youth.

But in 2008, all three of us checked the box for Obama, our votes helping deliver North Carolina to a Democratic presidential nominee for only the second time in forty years. My father had crossed party lines once before, in 1984, when Jesse Jackson ran for president. Jackson's business-size Afro, jet-black mustache, and Carolina preacher's staccato cadence transformed the typically all-white affair of presidential contests. "If a Black man had the opportunity to sit in the Oval

Office," my father told me years later, "I wasn't going to sit on the sidelines."

Jackson—who has the same fraternity letter, Ω, burned into his skin as my father and brother and me—championed a policy agenda nowhere close to my father's conservatism. But his rationale for supporting Jackson hinged on a basic proposition, informed by generations of Black experiences in America: the thousands of lesser decisions made in rooms of power can matter far more for racial equality than policy preferences. Vice President Kamala Harris captured this during her 2020 presidential campaign, saying it plainly: "It matters who's in those rooms."[1] My rationale for voting for the first time was much like my father's two decades earlier. I was not going to stand idly by if there was a chance to put a Black man in those rooms.

There isn't much of a story here. The Black folks voted for the Black guy. It didn't matter if one was a disengaged Black military officer, another the rare Black Republican, and the third a lifelong moderate Black Democrat. We did what everyone expected Black folks to do. David Carlin wrote in the Catholic magazine *Crisis* weeks before the 2008 election: "Of course, Black voters would vote overwhelmingly for any Democratic presidential candidate, not just Obama. But they will very probably vote even more overwhelmingly for Obama."[2]

Worse were the caricatures of Black Americans as self-absorbed and unthinking. When Colin Powell, a Republican and first Black chairman of the Joint Chiefs of Staff and first Black secretary of state, announced that he would be endorsing Obama, conservative talking head Rush Limbaugh criticized him for choosing race over "the nation and its welfare."[3] A few years later, he said Powell would vote for Obama again because "melanin is thicker than water."[4] Conservative pundit Pat Buchanan and others resurfaced the old and ugly allegation that Black people are trapped on the Democratic "plantation," tagging us as simpletons practicing a politics of grievance and welfare in exchange for votes.[5]

WHEN FOLKS SAY *Black people are not a monolith*, they are pushing back on the idea that Black people are a herd of voters who hold the same views on every policy and politician. The near uniformity of Black voting behavior, however, suggests a monolith of sorts does exist. The story is clearer in the numbers. From 1964 to 2008, an average of 88 percent of Black votes went to the Democratic Party's presidential nominees, a number that increased to 95 percent in the two elections when Obama was on the ballot, and 93 percent in the two elections after he left office.[6]

And yet just because Black people take similar votes doesn't mean they hold similar politics. Surveys routinely show our politics are scattered across the ideological spectrum. Just over two in five Black Americans identify as moderate and about a quarter each as liberal or conservative.[7] In several Southern states, nearly 40 percent of Black people say they're conservative.[8] The twist is that being white and conservative means you're probably voting Republican; being Black and conservative just means you have ideas about individualism, group self-reliance, or respectable behavior grounded in traditional African American religions . . . and most Black conservatives vote for Democrats.

Unity at the ballot box is not confirmation that Black voters hold the same views on every issue but that they hold the same view on the most consequential: racial equality. The Black electoral monolith only exists as evidence of a critical defect in America's practice of democracy. That defect is the space our two-party system makes for racial intolerance and the appetite our electoral politics has for the exploitation of racist ideas. The electoral solidarity of Black voters is an immune response.

It is, however, routinely misdiagnosed. In 2016, campaigning in a Michigan suburb that's 2 percent Black, Donald Trump prodded Black voters to give him a chance, asking: "What the hell do you have to lose?" He boasted to the nearly all-white audience: "At the end of four years, I guarantee you that I will get over 95 percent of the African American vote. I promise you."[9]

He did not. Instead, almost 95 percent voted *against* him. Then, in August 2020, Democratic presidential nominee Joe Biden said matter-of-factly that "unlike the African American community, with notable exceptions, the Latino community is an incredibly diverse community with incredibly different attitudes about different things."[10] That May he'd told the radio host Charlamagne tha God: "If you have a problem figuring out whether you're for me or Trump, then you ain't Black."[11]

These characterizations belie a more ominous reality: That Black Americans are canaries in the democratic coal mine, the first to detect when the air is foul. Signaling the danger that lies ahead.

• • •

TO BE BLACK IN AMERICA means to stand in political solidarity with other Black people. Authenticity is measured this way, a measure more important than one's party of policy preferences. Sometimes those politics are formal and electoral. Sometimes they are of protest and revolt. But they have always, by necessity, been either a matter of life and death or a people's reach for the civil liberties and social mobility that others have long enjoyed.

Black people's introduction to American democracy came via the cold calculus of the Constitution's Three-Fifths Compromise. The founders agreed we should be counted to help the states divvy up political power. But that we should not be fully counted so as not to give power to supporters of slavery. If you come from a people who are partially counted and wholly enslaved, it's natural to wonder whether a democracy like that can care about people like you. Democracy to enslaved people was little more than a negotiation on what other basic rights and wisps of liberty could be traded away. It seemed an instrument of oppression rather than a shield against it. Maybe other people would have used it differently.

When Black men were finally able to vote after the end of the Civil War, there seemed a binary choice: side with the party that supported your citizenship or with the one who would deny you those rights. Naturally, they supported Lincoln's racially progressive Republicans, who advocated for Black voting rights and representation. In 1867, more than 100,000 freed Black Virginian men registered to vote for delegates to the convention that would help facilitate the state's readmission to the Union. On the state's election day that October, 88 percent of them voted—many under the threat of being fired by their white employer—securing a supermajority of convention delegates for Republicans, more than a third of whom were Black.[12] The convention, filled by the electoral solidarity of Black voters and delegates, helped lead the state's successful reentry into the United States, formalize suffrage for freedmen, and extend civil rights.

The ratification of the Thirteenth, Fourteenth, and Fifteenth Amendments legally established freedmen's participation in the electoral process at a time when upward of 90 percent of Black people lived in the Southern states, constituting actual or near majorities in a few. This led to more than three hundred Black state and federal legislators in the South holding office in 1872, a level not seen again for more than a hundred years.[13] These elected officials were overwhelmingly Republicans swept into office by the unity of Black voters, who assembled to demand a liberty that hinged on keeping white segregationists from power.

In a healthy and thriving democracy, one aligned with the nation's professed values, competition for these new voters would've exploded. Democrats and Republicans alike would've recognized that winning elections meant earning Black voters' support. Both parties would have had to update their strategies, rethink the math. Competition would have chipped away at the monolith as individual Black voters sought out their ideological compatriots instead of being forced to make civil rights the only issue. Instead, race was made the issue anew.

It wasn't long before a campaign of white nationalist terrorism swept across the South, targeting Black Republican legislators and voters. In Georgia, the 1868 state legislature voted to expel its Black members, all of whom were Republicans. They were eventually reseated but not before racist vigilantes in the town of Camilla opened fire on Black marchers attending a party rally, killing, by some accounts, nearly a dozen and wounding dozens more.[14] That same year in South Carolina, white vigilantes killed a number of Black legislators. One of them, Benjamin F. Randolph, was shot in broad daylight at a train station.[15] No one was ever tried for the crime, let alone convicted of it. In the Colfax massacre of 1873, dozens of Black Republicans and state militiamen were killed on Easter Sunday when a gang of Ku Klux Klan members and former Confederate soldiers stormed the parish courthouse in an attempt to overturn election results in Louisiana.

Federal forces kept some of this racial terror in check. Some of it persisted. And white Republican leaders occasionally bowed to that violence out of political expedience. In the 1876 presidential election, nineteen electoral votes in three Southern states were disputed and accompanied by voter intimidation and widespread voter fraud. In South Carolina, voter turnout was an absurd 101 percent.[16] The moderate Republican presidential nominee Rutherford B. Hayes lost the popular vote but appeared to have an edge in winning the disputed electors. Republican Party leaders struck a deal with Democrats that would make Hayes president in exchange for a promise that federal troops would not intervene in Southern politics. Once in office, Hayes was a man of his word. The Compromise of 1877, as it is now known, effectively traded Black people's rights away for the keys to the White House. It brought Reconstruction to an end, paving the way for the Jim Crow era.

In the first century of American politics, the word *compromise*—Three-Fifths, Missouri, 1850, 1877—was often a euphemism for prying natural and constitutional rights from Black people. Perhaps betrayals of one group can be labeled compromises by the others, but racial hierarchy and equal rights cannot touch without bruising. These political arrangements underscored the paradox that plagued Black America from the outset: the same federalist government charged with the delivery and defense of constitutional rights was often the means of denying them. On matters of race, the state was at once dangerously unreliable and positively indispensable.

The contours of Black politics were shaped by this quandary. The lack of faith in American democracy's ability to do what was right undergirded Black conservatism, producing economic philosophies like Booker T. Washington's bootstrapping self-determination, social efforts toward civic acceptance like the respectability politics of the Black church, and separatist politics like the early iterations of Black nationalism and the Black Power movement. A recognition that achieving racial equality required a strong government fueled Black progressivism, which demanded anti-lynching federal legislation, eradication of the poll tax and other barriers to voting, and expansion of quality public education. Elections might have brought these strains of Black politics together out of necessity but did not erase the differences between them.

IN THE YEARS THAT FOLLOWED, the twin phenomena of the Great Migration and the Great Depression carried millions of Black Americans out of the South to new locales in search of physical and economic security, and by 1960 the share of the Black population residing outside of the Southern states had quadrupled to 40 percent. This influx of Black Americans led Northern and Midwestern white leaders and elected officials of both parties to devise campaign strategies and policy positions targeting Black voters.[17]

In the 1930s through the 1950s, that electoral solidarity was hardly a given. Democrats had a progressive economic agenda that appealed to Black voters, but the party was still home to the Southern conservatives ruthlessly enforcing Jim Crow laws. The Republican Party could have mounted a concerted national effort to keep Black voters by refusing to be outflanked on civil rights policies, but its coalition of pro-business interests was less enthusiastic about the regulatory compliance burden associated with civil rights measures on employment, wages, public accommodations, and housing.

Instead, Democratic national leadership made the first bold move. A year before the 1948 presidential election, noting the success of Franklin D. Roosevelt's New Deal electoral coalition, a campaign-strategy memo argued that "the Northern Negro voter today holds the balance of power in presidential elections for the simple arithmetical reason that the Negroes not only vote in a bloc but are geographically concentrated in pivotal, large and closely contested electoral states such as New York, Illinois, Pennsylvania, Ohio and Michigan."[18] Truman's decision to sign executive orders desegregating the military and the federal workforce was an electoral broadside constructed, in part, to help win over the support of Black Northern voters.

It worked. Truman won 77 percent of Black voters and with them the Great Migration destination states of Illinois and Ohio by just a combined 40,000 votes—and these states' electoral votes provided the margin of victory. The famous picture of the reelected president holding up the erroneous newspaper headline DEWEY DEFEATS TRUMAN exists in large part because Dewey, the Republican governor of New York with a solid record on civil rights, had grown suddenly lukewarm on the issue, making halfhearted appeals to Black voters in the North while increasing entreaties to white conservatives in the South.

The outcome of the 1948 election was proof of the new electoral advantage Black solidarity offered a party willing to deliver racially progressive policies. And the decision of many Southern Democrats, upset with the party's formal embrace of civil rights at that year's Democratic National Convention, to mount a third-party presidential bid was a tell. Disgruntled white segregationists were shopping for a new home.

The Democrats' and Republicans' national platforms in this period addressed civil rights in nearly equal measure. Sometimes Republicans were better. President Dwight D. Eisenhower declared in the 1950s that racial segregation harmed the nation's security interests. Deploying the 101st Airborne to enforce the integration of Little Rock Central High School in 1957, he warned that "our enemies are gloating over this incident and using it everywhere to misrepresent our whole nation."[19] Richard Nixon held positions on civil rights similar to John F. Kennedy's during the 1960 presidential campaign and won nearly a third of the Black vote that year (though in the South, where the majority of the Black population still lived, Black voters were effectively barred from the polls).

The Kennedy-Nixon contest was the last time a Republican would win more than 15 percent of the Black vote in a presidential election. Stumping for Nixon in 1960, Senator Barry Goldwater, the Arizona Republican, said about race issues, "There's hardly enough difference between Republican conservatives and the Southern Democrats to put a piece of paper between."[20] When Goldwater became the 1964 presidential nominee and voiced his opposition to the Civil Rights Act, Black voters bunched themselves into the Democratic Party for good, supporting Lyndon B. Johnson at a rate comparable with Barack Obama's nearly a half-century later.

The Voting Rights Act of 1965, meanwhile, greatly expanded the Black electorate—voter registration rates among nonwhites leapt to 59.8 percent in 1967 from 6.7 percent in Mississippi, to 51.6 percent from 19.3 percent in Alabama, and to 52.6 percent from 27.4 percent in Georgia. Black turnout soared.[21] And George Wallace's third-party candidacy for president in 1968, running on a segregation platform and winning five states in the process, was the last gasp for segregationists operating outside of the two-party system.

IF WE ARE BRAVE

Within a decade, white Southern Democrats were responding favorably to the appeals of the Republican Party's standard-bearers. Richard Nixon's "law and order" refrain and Ronald Reagan's renewed call for "states' rights" were racialized, arguing against progressive policies like busing and tapping into anxieties about a rapidly integrating society. With explicit racism now taboo, symbolic and colorblind gestures allowed discriminatory views to be cloaked in questions about free-market principles, personal responsibility, and small government. Racial segregation could be achieved without openly championing it; the social hierarchy maintained without evangelizing it. American voters, Black and white alike, got the message.

THE REPUBLICAN PARTY'S RIGHTWARD MOVE on race was a success, winning the White House in five out of six elections from 1968 to 1992. And the Senate in consecutive elections for the first time since the onset of the Great Depression. Meanwhile, the Democratic Party deepened its relationship with Black voters. The electoral power of Black voters produced historic firsts, like the first Black elected governor in the nation's history, Douglas Wilder of Virginia. Jesse Jackson lost his presidential primary runs in 1984 and 1988, but his strong showings won concessions in the Democratic Party platform. More Black members arrived in Congress, won mayoral races, and set the stage for the Black political identity to become synonymous with support for

Democrats. Symbolic fights, like over whether to commemorate Dr. Rev. Martin Luther King Jr. with a federal holiday, further clarified the racial divisions between the parties.

The result was that racial polarization was now less a product of political debates about the personhood or citizenship of Black Americans and more a fact of partisan identity. A political instrument to hold and wield power. This was a subtle but profound shift. And a dangerous one. Political scientist Lilliana Mason writes, "Partisan, ideological, religious, and racial identities have, in recent decades, moved into strong alignment, or have become 'sorted,'"[22] such that partisan attacks can become race-based, personal, and detached from policy fights.

So the parties don't compete for Black voters. They instead fight about the process of voting and about questions on whether it's easier or harder for Black folks to participate. The right to vote is less the fight today than access to the ballot box is. Local election officials in Georgia closed polling stations in many counties with large Black populations just before the 2018 gubernatorial election, leading to longer lines and lower turnout. Stacey Abrams fell just short of becoming the nation's first Black female governor. Republican-controlled legislatures in Texas, Alabama, and elsewhere passed voter-identification requirements that are twice as likely to complicate Black voters' access to the ballot as white voters'. Efforts to purge registration rolls in places like Wisconsin disproportionately affect Black voters. Both parties have gerrymandered congressional districts, reshaping Black electoral power. The voting-rights guardrails that are supposed to prevent these sorts of racially disparate complications have been mangled by hyperpartisanship and the courts.

Racial identity has now become fully entangled with partisanship: The Republican Party is attracting more white voters while people of color are massing in the Democratic Party. Scholars found that Black voters' desire to avoid being chastised for their politics by other Black people creates near-uniform support for Democrats, deemed to be the stronger party on important issues.[23] This affects white voters, too. Researchers learned that white people who associate the Democratic Party with Black people report a clear preference for the Republican Party. Race splits the parties more cleanly than ever, and the racial gap exacerbates partisan polarization.

The flaw in the American version of democracy that created the Black monolith—a tolerance for political incentives that foster racial division—is spawning others like it. The voting behaviors of Hispanic Americans and Asian Americans, groups that are growing more rapidly than any others, are trending in ways that resemble the Black electorate from nearly a century ago. Over the last several years, the two demographics have gone from relatively close splits between the two parties in presidential elections to at least two-thirds of each now voting for the Democratic nominee. Today more than eight in ten Black Americans identify as Democratic or Democratic-leaning, and more than a third of the party's members of Congress are people of color. Only half of white Americans identify with Republicans, but they account for eight in ten members of the party. And 95 percent of congressional Republicans are white; as of 2024, only five are Black.

The modern American two-party system so consecrates competition that party leaders are more incentivized to disparage the other side as extreme and un-American than to compromise. When Trump had a dispute with four Democratic congresswomen of color, he said of the women during a White House news conference: "They hate our country. They hate it, I think, with a passion."[24] Nancy Pelosi, a Democrat and then–Speaker of the House, had chastised Trump the day before on social media, asserting: "When @realDonaldTrump tells four American Congresswomen to go back to their countries, he reaffirms his plan to 'Make America Great Again' has always been about making America white again."[25] The line between partisanship and racial conflict has thinned. In *How Democracies Die*, Harvard professors Steven Levitsky and Daniel Ziblatt argue that when elected officials use the instruments of government to divide and polarize the public, destabilize institutions, and demonize opponents, they can send a democracy into a death spiral.

If this process begins at the ballot box, perhaps it can be halted there, too. Maybe other people will use it differently.

From its earliest days, Black solidarity has been as an act of self-preservation, not an attempt to be saviors of American democracy. But it understands that inclusion in the latter is the only means to secure the former.

• • •

IN MY CHILDHOOD HOME DURING the summer after George Floyd's murder, I sat with my parents in an animated discussion about the two dozen men and women—of varying ages, races, ethnicities, ideologies, socioeconomic statuses, and experiences—who had hoped to secure the Democratic presidential nomination in 2020. The orientation of the house politics had not changed much over the decades. My father, who could not stomach the current version of the Republican Party, held on to a conservatism pulling in equal measure from Booker T. Washington's philosophy of self-help and the Black Power's racial pride and suspicion of government. My mother was less willing to let government off the hook and insisted that it deliver on the race-conscious promises of equal protection promised in the Constitution.

In a way, there was little daylight between them; each wanted nothing more than a level playing field and for their individual efforts to pay off fairly. One chose the belief that government should work to remove the discriminatory obstacles hindering Black America while the other believed it should ensure the advantages enjoyed by white America are available to us, too. I suppose my politics were the nation should do both, but that it has been loath to commit to either. And that it will probably be this way for a while.

That evening we discussed the candidates' differing approaches to healthcare, how (or whether) they talked about racial economic disparities, the importance of criminal justice and education reforms, and who among the contenders had the best chance at winning the White House. When the conversation ended and the tenor of the house mellowed—cable news replaced with soul music, soul food, and laughter that's good for the soul—I was glad we'd reached no consensus.

Deliberation is the lifeblood of a healthy democracy. A people that does not seriously deliberate about its nation and its leaders is a people ill-suited to the task of keeping government in check. For Black voters, full agency and electoral freedom remain luxuries.

It didn't have to be this way. There have been moments in history in which better leaders and better people would have competed for Black America's increasing electoral power instead of organizing against it. Rutherford B. Hayes could have strengthened the presence of federal troops in the South and kept Democrats' sanctioned racial terrorism at bay. Dewey could have refused to exchange leadership on civil rights for support from business interests and Southern conservatives. The Republican Party could have followed through on its own calls for party diversification after losing the 2012 presidential election instead of lurching in the opposite direction. But for a nation deeply divided on race relations, the easy and more politically expedient strategy has always won out.

We will know our nation is on the right path toward building a healthier and more resilient democracy when the Black monolith erodes. Should Black Americans ever secure the freedom to vote according to their politics instead of against those who believe civil rights protections are excessive and burdensome, it will signal that our country has discovered an elusive resolve, the one required to overcome the historical effects of racism on our society.

For our democracy to reach its final form, the answer cannot be that one party tried to answer the call—it must be that each party does so and without penalty. A young John Lewis made this argument in 1963 at the foot of the Lincoln Memorial. In his impassioned speech, he channeled the frustrations of Black America and excoriated the nation's partisan democracy for posturing on race relations instead of taking revolutionary action to realize the promise of America. His rhetorical questions still ring true today as racial tensions remain very much alive: "Where is the political party that will make it unnecessary to march on Washington?"[26]

The voting behavior of Black people will tell us when, if ever, this occurs.

THEODORE R. JOHNSON

PART II: SENATORS

In January 1870, people in the nation's capital—white and Black—were curious to get a look at the city's newest arrival: the Mississippi legislator Hiram Rhodes Revels. He'd traveled for days by steamboat and train, forced into the "Colored" sections by captains and conductors, en route to becoming the first Black senator in United States history.

Not long after Revels's train pulled into the New Jersey Avenue Station in Washington, DC, the city's Black folks had gathered and cheered the man who'd made history. Newspaper articles chronicled his every step as he made his rounds of the city's elite. The reports were detailed. One reporter noted Revels was well appointed in a sharp black suit and a neat beard beneath cheekbones fresh off a razor. There were lunches with leading civil rights advocates; daily congratulatory visits from as many as fifty men at the Capitol Hill home where he was the guest of a prominent Black Republican; and exclusive interracial soirees hosted by Black businessmen, including the president of the Freedman's Savings Bank.

Senators were eager to meet him, too. Mississippi's seats in the Senate had been vacant since 1861, when it seceded from the Union and its members resigned. One of them was Jefferson Davis, who gave a farewell address in that august chamber and, exactly four weeks later, was inaugurated as president of the Confederacy. Revels's election was the

48

product of newly enfranchised freedmen who'd voted 115 Black people into Mississippi's legislature.[27] In those days, the state representatives picked who their United States senators would be. Those newly elected Black men, enslaved just years earlier, chose a Black man to take the place of a man who left to go fight for the right to enslave Black people. Justice is sometimes poetic.

Before Revels could be sworn in and officially seated, Mississippi had to be readmitted into the Union. So he busied himself with visits to his nephew in Baltimore, attending dinners and parties held in his honor, and repeatedly returning to the Senate to check on progress. Word of the "new Negro senator" quickly spread across the country, filling newspaper columns and American imaginations. Philadelphia's *Evening Telegraph* described him as a "thick-set mulatto, with a decidedly African but pleasant physiognomy, and bland, agreeable manner," which is a trip.[28] The Black press brimmed with praise; *New Era*, one of Washington's weeklies, cited Revels's patriotism for his service in the Union Army and declared him "a wonderful improvement, in loyalty at least, upon Jefferson Davis."[29]

Other outlets were less charitable. The *Public Ledger* in Memphis, Tennessee: "The negro, aside from the disgrace of being such, is an unmitigated scoundrel."[30] The *Chicago Republican* went further, suggesting that the new senator's race "brings into prominence, as a practical question of great interest and importance, the issue of his eligibility."[31] In other words, though Revels was born in the United States, Black people weren't considered citizens until after the ratification of the Fourteenth Amendment in 1868. The argument was that Revels hadn't been a citizen long enough to be eligible for office. The ugly insinuation at the heart of the charge reveals the nation's defining challenge. Revels presented to an adolescent nation—still climbing out from the rubble of the Civil War—the question of when Black people became American.

On February 23, weeks after Revels's arrival, Mississippi was formally readmitted into the United States, and that meant Revels could finally take his seat in the Senate. Just as the chamber was preparing to swear him in, Willard Saulsbury, a senator from Delaware, objected; other senators soon joined, citing the Constitution's requirement that a person must be a citizen of the United States for at least nine years before becoming a senator. The Supreme Court's 1857 decision in *Dred Scott v. Sandford* determined that Black people could not be citizens, and the Fourteenth Amendment's enactment of birthright citizenship had only recently been established. The recalcitrant senators argued that Revels was ineligible because he could claim, at most, two years of American citizenship.

The Senate engaged in a fiery debate for parts of three days, with Revels taking it all in from a seat in the chamber while his colleagues carried on about him as if only the furniture were there. Beneath the veneer of competing readings

IF WE ARE BRAVE

of the Constitution lay another unavoidable question that continues to test America's first principles: Can a democracy shaped by Black participation be legitimate?

• • •

AFTER THE PRESIDENTIAL ELECTION IN 2020, on the very floor where Revels's citizenship and eligibility were debated 150 years earlier, dissenting senators rose again to question the legitimacy of a duly elected Black person. This time it was whether a Black senator, Kamala Harris, could be seated as the nation's first Black vice president. The date was January 6, 2021.

The night before, the same Black voters whose high turnout and overwhelming support helped Joe Biden and Kamala Harris win the state of Georgia did something else. They helped Rev. Raphael Warnock win a runoff election to become just the eleventh Black US senator in history and only the second Black senator from the South since Reconstruction.

But within a few hours, the news of his victory and its significance was drowned out as a violent horde—seditious rioters, insurrectionists—attacked the Capitol, following President Trump's exhortations to "take back our country."[32] In the same building that Jefferson Davis once defiantly exited in order to wage war against the United States, and on the same day the Senate was set to send one Black member to the vice presidency and gain its first Black member from the state of Georgia, an insurrection swelling with white nationalists paraded the Confederate battle flag through the halls of Congress.

Everything old is new again.

REVELS'S PATH TO THE UNITED STATES SENATE coursed through the sacred pulpits of the Black church and the towering bluffs of a military encampment along the Mississippi River. He was born free in North Carolina in 1827, was educated in religious schools, and then became a teacher and minister in the Methodist church. Though he was a free Black man in the era of slavery, his skin color, more than his status, stamped his American experience. He traveled extensively, teaching and preaching to free and enslaved Black people alike, being careful to avoid language in his sermons that a monitoring white public might interpret as inciting rebellion.

As the nation descended into war, Revels contributed to the Union cause wherever he could, first raising a Black work battalion in Maryland and then an all-Black regiment in Missouri. By 1864, he had joined the Union Army as a chaplain and went to Mississippi to minister to Black soldiers there who had bravely fought at Vicksburg, a battle that helped put an end to the lie that "the negro won't fight."[33] With the war decided and slavery abolished, newly freed Black Americans found the early days of Reconstruction full of hope and trouble.

The promise of life free from bondage was quickly met by a violent resistance to Black people acting like they were free. Black Codes were enacted across the Southern states as white authorities sought to reassert the racial order that the war had disrupted. Vagrancy laws were weaponized to force Black people into exploitive labor agreements and incentivized white surveillance of their movements and activities. And yet states seeking readmission into the Union had to give Black people the vote in order to be readmitted. The expansion of American democracy to accommodate Black participation was a threat to the understanding that democracy in America was two things: man's work and whites-only.

In the years immediately following the war, Revels returned to Mississippi to lead a Methodist church. Recognized for his intelligence and easygoing nature, he was elected to his first political office as an alderman in 1868. He landed in the state assembly the next year and at the heart of the debate about Black Americans' citizenship eighteen months after he entered politics.

• • •

THE LONELY WALKS OF THE Black senator begin here. Two days after senators argued about whether American democracy ever intended there to be a Black senator, on February 25, 1870, Hiram Revels was finally sworn into the Senate on a party-line vote. The Republican Party of Lincoln supported the seating. The Democratic Party, then home to white nationalists, opposed it.

A crowd had assembled in the Senate galleries to get a glimpse of this moment when a Black American took national office. The onlookers were so electric and the moment so polarizing that the vice president chairing the session had to reprimand those in attendance for their impassioned "manifestations of feeling." The *New York Herald* described a suffocating anxiety in the room as Revels approached the clerk to take his oath of office, "as if the appearance of some monster was expected in the Senate chamber."[34] The *Cincinnati Daily Enquirer* found its monster. The next day, its headline read THE MISSISSIPPI GORILLA ADMITTED TO THE SENATE. Revels served just a year in the Senate, completing the special term to which he was elected. But the Mississippi legislature elected another Black man to the Senate.

Blanche Bruce, the son of an enslaved Black woman and a white man who considered her his property, is the only American to have gone from slavery to the Senate. His political ascendance paralleled a fracture in the state's Republican Party over the issue of Black citizenship—one side checking out of the fight for civil rights and the other increasingly uninterested in making nice with white segregationists. Bruce, imposing and barrel-chested, aligned himself with this second group and won a full term in the Senate. He immediately went to work. He fought for benefits for Black veterans, tried to desegregate the US Army, was an advocate for Native American equality, opposed the Chinese Exclusion Act, and even demanded an investigation into the racist hazing of the Black West Point cadet Johnson C. Whittaker.

By the time Bruce's term ended in 1881, so had Reconstruction. With federal troops no longer enforcing civil rights protections, white segregationists violently and methodically retook the South. In the part of the country where more than 90 percent of Black Americans lived, racial terrorism and measures like grandfather clauses, poll taxes, and literacy tests kept them out of voting booths and elected office. Black people were intentionally and systematically removed from the democracy.

Eight decades. That's how long it would take before the Senate seated another Black person. As millions of Black Americans left the South in the Great Migration in search of economic and physical security, the political opportunities that slowly became available would include the House of Representatives. The Senate remained out of reach.

THE 1966 ELECTION OF THE Massachusetts Republican Edward Brooke to the Senate broke the embarrassing streak. After the passage of the Civil Rights Act of 1964 and the Voting Rights Act of 1965, Brooke's victory was significant not just because of his race but because he was a Republican at a time when the party had begun courting disaffected

Southern Democrats. The Black Power movement was just getting underway. Aggressive demands for racial equality became more common, challenging the respectability politics of the Civil Rights Movement. Brooke, a World War II veteran, represented a palatable version of Blackness to a skittish nation.

His politics, an evolution of those practiced by Revels and Bruce a century earlier, would come to be the playbook for every Black senator that came after him. Brooke toed the line on race consciousness and colorblind conservatism, declaring: "I do not intend to be a national leader of the Negro people. I intend to do my job as a senator from Massachusetts."[35] But he was no partisan yes-man. He refused to support, or even be photographed with, the 1964 Republican presidential nominee, Barry Goldwater, who opposed that year's Civil Rights Act and dog-whistled his way through the South by championing states' rights. He shot down two of President Nixon's Supreme Court nominees because of their backward-looking civil rights views. And he was the first Republican to call for Nixon's resignation following the Watergate scandal.

When Brooke left the Senate in January 1979, a political language had emerged that eerily invoked the period after Reconstruction: *law and order*, often a euphemism for maintaining racial order; *states' rights*, as cover for skirting civil rights protections in the Constitution; *personal responsibility*, an evasion of the systemic economic subjugation of Black

Americans. In this way, any policy issue—school desegregation, unemployment rates, housing, criminal justice—could be discussed in colorblind terms while still producing, intentionally or not, the cumulative effect of making Black people's lives more difficult than they should have been.

In the forty years following the end of Brooke's term—1979 to 2019—the Senate had only seven Black members who were appointed by their state's governor to fill vacancies. Until 2021, all but one were from states outside the South: South Carolina's Tim Scott is the first since Reconstruction and remains the only Republican.

The progress of the twenty-first century, however, would run headlong into the haunting racism of the nineteenth. The rapid rise of Senators Barack Obama and Kamala Harris to the national stage, accompanied by the growing electoral influence of Black Americans, resurrected white reactionary backlash. It manufactured a crisis of legitimacy by questioning the eligibility of Obama and Harris for the highest offices in the land. The Senate debate about Hiram Revels a century and a half ago is from the same strain of racism as the birtherism conspiracy that trailed Obama during his campaign and once he was in office—and which was used by Donald Trump to boost his own political fortunes. Distorted readings of the Fourteenth Amendment challenged whether Harris, the daughter of immigrants from Jamaica and India, was eligible to be vice president.

In a noteworthy turn of history, former senator Joe Biden

of Delaware—who served as vice president to the first Black president and now serves as president with the first Black vice president—occupied the same Senate seat as Willard Saulsbury, the man who first objected to seating Revels in 1870. The echoes of eras past resound in present-day America, where Black Americans' participation in the nation's leadership is seen by some not as a fulfillment of its founding ideals but as an existential threat to them.

This is the history that Raphael Warnock stepped into when he declared his run for the Senate in 2020. His Republican opponent, a white woman, ran a political ad that darkened Warnock's skin, accused him of being a "Marxist radical," and combed through his sermons to find language that proved Warnock harbored "anti-American hatred." The day before voters were set to choose between her and Warnock, President Trump declared, "Warnock is the most radical and dangerous left-wing candidate ever to seek this office, and certainly in the state of Georgia, and he does not have your values."[36]

. . .

COTTON, AS THE OLD FOLKS SAY, is hell to pick. When the soft white tufts burst through, they conceal the seeds buried inside and the sharp bolls in which they sit. The harvest comes in late summer, when the Southern humidity is at its most oppressive. Enslaved Black people often spoke of the pain coming and going—greeting you in the fingertips from the barbed bolls and chasing you in the sun's unblinking heat on your back and the fear of an overseer's lash. Over time those hands grew callused and a little bit more resilient. For Black Americans, the picking has often been prickly business.

Warnock summoned this history in the emotional opening moments of his victory speech. Reflecting on his mother's teenage days picking cotton to eke out a living in rural Waycross, Georgia, Warnock captured the progress of a people and a nation in a single sentence: "Because this is America, the eighty-two-year-old hands that used to pick somebody else's cotton went to the polls and picked her youngest son to be a United States senator."[37]

Tim Scott, a lifelong resident of South Carolina, has highlighted the same journey within his own family. He often notes that his grandfather could not read or write after being forced out of third grade to pick cotton. But he lived to see his grandson elected to both the House and the Senate. "Our family went from cotton to Congress in one lifetime."[38] It is the phrase Scott cannot afford to leave alone. He is an overzealous member of the Republican caucus in the Senate. Once circumspect, he managed to talk forthrightly about race at times while signaling to a wary nation that he is not an extremist. In one instant he is declining to join the Congressional Black Caucus, and in the next he is holding court on the Senate floor for three days in one week on the problem of racism in America.

He tells the nation, from the very floor that once questioned whether his skin forbade his citizenship, that he'd been racially profiled by the Capitol Police while wearing the Senate lapel pin that belongs only to members—and how the officer stated, "with a little attitude" as Scott recalled, "The pin I know. You, I don't. Show me your ID."[39] Political ambitions, however, led him to throw away such cautions. These days, he seems a loyal partisan, to the point of caricature, above all else.

Warnock, who grew up in the housing projects of Savannah as the eleventh child of Pentecostal preachers, has had to navigate this same troubled landscape. He's had to balance a certain sense of responsibility to the race with the prestige of an office allergic to assertions of Black agency. The intrinsically American Puritan work ethic he inherited from his army veteran father and his deep admiration for the Rev. Dr. Martin Luther King Jr. kept him focused on his education. He decided to attend Morehouse College, the historically Black all-male institution in Atlanta, just as King did. Warnock leveraged the pulpit of the Black church to advocate for policy. He started out as a youth pastor at the historic Abyssinian Baptist Church in New York City and ascended to become senior pastor of Ebenezer Baptist Church in Atlanta, the same house of worship where King preached and is buried. Along the way, he encouraged Black clergy members and others in the community to be tested for HIV when many were wary, pressed for criminal justice

IF WE ARE BRAVE

reforms, and even went to jail. In 2017 he was arrested without incident during a peaceful demonstration in a US Senate office building for protesting efforts to repeal the Affordable Care Act.

In the course of seeking office, Warnock recognized the unique obstacles and hazards that Black politicians and Democrats face in Southern states that have been reliably Republican for decades. He needed to increase Black turnout by making implicit appeals to the benefits of representation, champion a progressive policy agenda to win over white liberals, and accentuate his everyday Americanness so as not to trigger the racial sensitivities of a capricious white public. Warnock's political ads featuring a cute little beagle took direct aim at those attempts to cast him as ill-suited to represent Georgia in the Senate, suggesting that he was incompatible with the culture of real Americans and a danger to democracy.

In one ad, he is seen strolling down a neighborhood sidewalk with the beagle and affectionately cradling the dog while dressed in the uniform of the American suburbs—a blue button-down shirt underneath an outdoorsy vest. "I think Georgians will see her ads for what they are," Warnock says of his opponent's attacks. With a genial smile, he drops a bag of dog poo in a trash can and then turns to the beagle to ask, "Don't you?"[40] Political scientists noted that the ads were a subtle but powerful rebuttal to the insinuations about his values and sensibilities—and to the stereotypes and hysteria that shadow Black men, even those who are pastors and hold public office. He was telling Georgians, "Despite what you might have heard, I share your values."

On January 5, 2021, Warnock won a special election runoff to become the eleventh Black senator in American history. A couple of years later, the twelfth, Laphonza Butler, was appointed to fill the seat of California senator Dianne Feinstein, who passed away in office. In the last forty years, Illinois has been home to three: Carol Moseley Braun, the first Black woman to be a US senator; Barack Obama; and Roland Burris. Two from California, Harris and Butler. Cory Booker of New Jersey and Mo Cowan of Massachusetts (whose appointment to the office lasted just five months) fill out the lonely group. It was only in 2012 that, for the first time in the nation's history, the Senate had more than one Black member. Of the eight Black senators this century, four were initially seated by appointment and two via special election. The remaining two, who both won a statewide election in a regular election cycle: President Barack Obama and Vice President Kamala Harris.

ON THE SUNDAY AFTER HIS ELECTION TRIUMPH, and after Trump supporters invaded the Capitol in a deadly threat to politicians, police officers, and democracy itself, Warnock delivered a sermon. "Just as we were trying to put on our celebration shoes," Warnock lamented, "the ugly side of our story, our great and grand American story, began to emerge."[41] Like Revels before him, Warnock's sense of justice and his understanding of the fullness of the Black experience had been crystallized during his time leading congregations, and his religious faith served to bolster his devotion to the American project. The nation had come so far from those perilous years after the Civil War and yet perhaps not so very far at all.

"As we consider what happened—the ugliness of it all—I want us to recognize that we didn't see in that moment the emergence of violence," Warnock said. "I want you to see the ways in which the violence was already there."[42]

CHAPTER 3

Is Democracy for White People?

Joining the military was never the plan. When high school graduation arrived, I knew exactly who, what, and where I wanted to be later in life. I remember all those specifics from decades ago because teenage me—Teddy—scribbled them into a high school senior memory book, a puffed hardcover journal that was part diary and part scrapbook. The cover was the splash of brightly colored blocks that defined the early nineties. Inside, the pages were full of prompts and questions to help capture what life was like in your graduation year. Your happiest and scariest moments. The cost of a movie ticket (I wrote $4.50) or a gallon of gas ($1.10). Class superlatives. A whole page for that "special someone" that I had to paper over with a new girl because teenage love can be a fickle thing. Alongside my chicken-scratch handwriting in blue and black ink are pictures from prom, a name tag from the afterschool job where I bagged groceries and stocked shelves, college acceptance letters, and even a newspaper clipping about the death of a classmate.

On pages ten and eleven, where the book asks for predictions of life five and ten years after graduation, the daydreams of an introverted teenager hoping to have a successful career are laid bare. At the five-year mark, I wrote my professional status as "a biomedical engineer on my way to a master's degree," graduated from Duke University and driving a "small sports car or midsize sports sedan." At year ten? I'd be working for a "major corporation designing artificial limbs" and living in a major Southern city "like Atlanta, Richmond, or New Orleans" while making "$70,000 but no less than $50,000" and vacationing at "my beach home in South Carolina or Florida." Most importantly, I was going to be fine: "tall, bowlegged, muscular, and very smart"—the word *very* was underlined twice. The military was nowhere to be found.

Old folks say that if you want to make God laugh, tell him your plans. Well, I didn't get into Duke, and I don't have an engineering degree. I neither embarked on a career designing artificial limbs nor whipped a sports car around Atlanta or New Orleans after graduation. I have not grown since high school, and I did not get fine. Instead, my bowlegged and pigeon-toed self followed scholarship money to Hampton University, the historically Black college that we affectionately call our Home by the Sea. I sat on that waterfront on many days, struggling with time management and wondering why math was mostly letters and words and not numbers.

The whole thing was all quite Huxtable.

During my freshman year of college, the officer in charge of US Navy recruiting in Raleigh, North Carolina, moved into the house across the street from my parents and, upon finding out that they had a kid in college, left a bunch of materials about a new Navy program intended to diversify its officer ranks. Though I previously had no real desire to be in the military, the thought that I could collect a paycheck while in college, have a guaranteed job after graduation, and embark on a career that would make my parents proud (and keep me off their couch) was all the convincing I needed. I headed to the Navy's officer candidate school in Pensacola, Florida, to be exercised into a ball of agony and sweat by Marine Corps drill instructors. Here is where my teenage dreams came partially true: those military barracks along the bay are likely as close as I'll ever get to having a beach home in Florida. That's God teasing.

A year later, I was at my first military assignment in San Diego. There I trained for six-month deployments on ships traveling through the Pacific and Indian Oceans to enforce United Nations sanctions in the Arabian Gulf against Saddam Hussein's Iraq. As a newly commissioned officer on a ship with about three hundred people, I led a team of seven sailors to collect intelligence, help identify oil-smuggling cargo vessels, and detect any threats to our crew.

Part of earning the job qualification was going on two-week training trips at sea with a more experienced officer to learn the art of leadership, get more familiar with the classified equipment we were responsible for, and understand how to navigate life on a ship. I was paired with a guy named John, who I soon learned had no business training anyone to do much of anything. Except how to irk. Even my bosses knew this—after we returned from the short deployment, one of them pulled me aside and said, "Forget everything you learned from him." I didn't need to be told twice. I'd already taken the experience with John and tossed it overboard as soon as the ship returned to San Diego.

Except for the one conversation that I keep with me.

On deployments, gathered in tight spaces when things are slow, two kinds of sailors emerge: the funny guy and the shit-starter. John was not funny. So when the topic of alma maters came up and I mentioned my HBCU, his eyes brightened. A little smirk danced on the corner of his mouth as he huffed, "A Blacks-only school, huh?"

Oh Lord, here we go.

"I've always wondered why those schools even exist," he snarled. "Segregation is over. Blacks can go to any college they can get into. What's the point of having Blacks-only schools anymore?"

The way he kept saying *Blacks* bothered me. I went into an immediate pro-HBCU defense, but within a few sentences, it was clear from his glazing-over eyes that there was no interest. He'd made up his mind, and now the point was to be right. Rather than risk turning this into a confrontation, I tried to move the conversation along. He was having none of it.

"All I know is that those schools are racist."

"WHAT?!"

I had to check myself. And remember where we were—the military has little tolerance for disrespecting a senior officer. Taking a breath, I asked, "How are HBCUs racist??"

"They're Blacks-only. White people can't even go to them."

"That's not true! Who told you that? Not only can y'all go there, you can get diversity scholarships! Instead of paying an arm and an asshole to go to your little fancy university, maybe you could've gotten a scholarship and gone to an HBCU."

"Yeah, okay. But why the hell would I wanna do that??"

And there it was.

Nothing left to argue about, really. The idea of being in a world filled with Black people—living with them, eating with them, learning from them, seeing them in every room and around every corner—was more than unimaginable to him. It was undesirable.

Even a world full of the good Huxtable ones.

There was no incentive that would make it appealing. He had no interest in such a place, not even temporarily and not even when it was confined to a college campus and not even

IF WE ARE BRAVE

if his career choice would not have been affected (after all, our different colleges landed us in the exact same job). The thought of being in it at all was too much.

. . .

FOR SOME NUMBER OF WHITE AMERICANS, the election of Barack Obama changed the country—for the worse. Not because of concerns about how he'd handle healthcare reforms or the social safety net or national security or the economy. These particular folks were worried that white people were losing their place in America. And the status and meaning that came with it. The visual of a Black family in the White House signaled a change, a move away from traditional conceptions of who Americans were, what they looked like, and the culture they forged. For whatever people think of presidents and the White House, they are symbols that embody the country's democratic identity. From Andrew Jackson and Woodrow Wilson, Theodore Roosevelt to Richard Nixon and Jimmy Carter, to understand why Americans selected a particular president is to understand who Americans believe they are, aspire to be, or want to avoid becoming. Sometimes that means embracing change and progress, sometimes it means rejecting them and insisting on maintaining the status quo, and sometimes it means revanchism and turning back the clock.

Obama's victory was a political loss for Republicans, but

that was secondary by a country mile to the symbolic loss many white people felt. The emergence of the Tea Party movement—funded by elites who hijacked a national myth—was due in large part to this sense that status had been lost. It breathed life into birtherism conspiracies about Obama's nationality before fueling the rise of Trumpism just a few years later. While the movement claimed its focus was on reducing the national debt and decreasing government spending, neither of those things happened once Republicans held the White House and Congress from 2017 to 2019. The Trump administration's budget shortfalls crossed the trillion-dollar mark, putting him in the top three of presidents with the largest budget deficits.[1] So we know what they were really mad about.

What knitted the movement together and clothed Trumpism was racial resentment, which is the idea that people of color—Black folks in particular—are culturally inferior, resist hard work and individualism, and should not benefit from government programs that address inequality. Studies repeatedly show that a Black man in the White House sent this resentment soaring, becoming the engine for an Americanism that rejects new leaders from newer citizens.

But careful. This is not the same thing as hatred, as being "racist in your heart." Accusing a Tea Party member or Trump supporter, for example, of judging people because of their skin will be met with proof of real relationships with the very people they're said to hate. It's possible to resent, and maybe be afraid of, rapid changes in the country's people and leadership without hating the people responsible for the change. You can be socially conservative and not Republican. The problem is not a partisan one.

THE EXPERIENCES OF TWO FRIENDS capture the complicated ways that racial resentment works in our democracy. The first friend is a former colleague who volunteered on the Obama campaign in 2008 and was canvassing a neighborhood in central Pennsylvania, the part of the country where the houses are mostly three-story duplexes with narrow driveways and power lines stretching across the street like circus wires. The people are white and working-class and culturally conservative. Rusting gutters and fading paint on small porches frame pale American flags, the color beaten out by the sun and rain. Every so often a barking dog has a word. One of the canvassers recounted an interaction with one pair of residents, revealing a side of racial politics in the United States that he'll never forget.

After the canvassers knocked on the door and waited a few seconds, a middle-aged white woman appeared and listened as they explained who they were and why they were there. When asked if she knew who her choice for president was, she turned her head to the side and yelled her husband's name into the house. When he responded, she said, "Who are we voting for president?" He yelled his reply, loud enough for those outside to hear: "The nigger."

When my colleague mouthed the word, my mouth dropped.

The woman didn't repeat it. She just said they'd be supporting Obama. Despite the coarse language, is it progress if the racists vote for the Black guy? Maybe they preferred the Democrats' economic policy, which would track with traditional white Northern working-class populist politics. Maybe party mattered more than person. Or maybe they thought Joe Biden—the kid from Scranton who became a senator before joining Obama's ticket as vice president—would make sure things were okay. We'll never know. For the canvassers, the point was to get Obama elected, not bicker about language that people use in their homes.

Take that scene with this one. A friend overheard a conversation between his father and his father's friend. My buddy comes from a connected family that's been engaged in the Democratic Party for decades at the local and national levels. They religiously attend the Democratic National Convention and rub elbows with leaders in the party establishment. So when Joe Biden won the Democratic primary in 2020 and selected Kamala Harris as his running mate, there was no question that the Biden-Harris ticket would receive their support.

When my friend's father had people over to his house

just before the election, one of the guests was not that enthusiastic about Harris being part of the administration.
It wasn't because of her time as a district attorney or as
California's attorney general. It wasn't because of policies
she championed as a senator. And it wasn't because her per-
sonality grated his nerves or that he believed all the salacious
rumors about her political ascendance. He left nothing to
the imagination as to why he didn't approve of Harris as
vice president: "I don't like that Black bitch being one heart
attack away from the presidency."

If those are the words from someone who voted *for her*,
are the lengths that those who voted against her might go
to really surprising? Just to prevent her from being a breath
away from being the face of the nation?

The United States of America is a woman of color. Too many
of our countrymen would rather burn things than let that
be true.

● ● ●

IS DEMOCRACY FOR WHITE PEOPLE? It's a rhetorical question
meant to be a provocation, but it's a good question, none-
theless. The country's biggest internal fights are usually over
who can belong, who can participate. Once new people battle
their way into democratic citizenship, they soon show up in
the halls of power. It's one thing to let others participate in
your system. It's something else to give them control over it

and your destinies, too. Being hesitant to change is human, reasonable. But when the response is backlash and exclusion directed at a people, the true nature of the objection is revealed. Race and gender soon show themselves.

Consider the vote. It's the basic unit of democracy. The right to vote serves as a state's boundary—those who can cast a ballot are in; those who cannot are confined to the outer limits. It's one of the first indications our country gives a previously excluded people that their status has truly changed. Historically, it was a right reserved for the few, effectively making it a privilege based on arbitrary factors: race, class, and gender. Millions of Black men became eligible to vote following the post–Civil War constitutional amendments, changing the parties' electoral calculus and the outcome of elections. It was an unwelcome change for many, so their strategy of keeping these new voters away from American democracy shifted from denying the right to vote to denying the ability to exercise that right. Easy access to the ballot box became democracy's newest privilege. Like today.

Policing who participates in our democracy is less about stinginess with voting rights and its privileges than it is about determining who can win office. Voting access is toyed with so much because the side that can shape who votes has more influence over who leads, over who makes the decisions. If the balance of power between the parties and the states had remained unchanged once all those new Black voters cast ballots after the Civil War, opposition to their participation would've been far less political. The problem wasn't that they changed the system of democracy; it was that they changed its victors.

New voters are disruptive because they put new people in office. And the expectation is that elected officials from groups long excluded will arrive to advocate for policies that help their communities in particular. Their wins, it will be said, come at the expense of those who've been in the democracy much longer. The classic voters see the new ones as a threat. This scene plays out along racial and partisan lines—generational, gender, and ideological ones, too. Intraparty squabbles pit hard-liners against the moderates. When a democratic people sees large groups of their countrymen as political threats, crisis is inevitable. We do not agree on who should lead because we do not agree on who can.

We come by this trait honestly. In our nation's mythology, American democracy was the creation of enlightened men. These architects crafted a nation out of ideas about equality and representation and assigned the privilege of voting to a select few made in their image: propertied white men. As the democracy expanded to integrate new people—immigrants from Europe to Asia, the indigent, non-Christians, formerly enslaved Black people, women, Indigenous peoples, and so on—that image was made sacrosanct and central to the American identity. A diverse democracy is fine as long as it's a republic where real Americans lead. As long as the myth remains intact.

• • •

AS POLITICAL POWER BECOMES AVAILABLE to more people, the old stories aren't good enough anymore. Multiracial democracies have trouble finding a shared story because of how central race is to their particular histories. Core myths become points of contention. They are tested most in those moments when new voters rush in and new leaders from people long outcast emerge, forcing national identity, ideas about race, and democracy-for-whom questions to collide. The nation's responses in these moments—and how they are remembered—tell us how race has shaped who should have access to democracy. Who should vote, who should lead. Who are the most American and who can become so. Will the country make room?

The first two major expansions of voting rights in the United States tell a story. One occurred in the early 1800s when the vote was granted to previously excluded white men. Voting eligibility in those days hinged on four things: gender, age, race, and property. Sometimes religion was added in as a requirement. In Maryland, voters were required to be Christian. States like South Carolina and New Jersey only allowed men "professing a belief in the faith of any Protestant sect"[2] to hold office. The demographic password for democracy was a propertied white Christian man of age. All others must wait for his grace.

But in the 1820s, parties identified the political advantage in making voting accessible to white men more generally. The land, tax-paying, and religious requirements mostly fell away. Some studies suggest the number of white male voters nearly tripled between 1824 and 1828. Others offer that the expansion in the wake of Jackson's presidency is overstated.[3] But we know white populist voters came in waves to Andrew Jackson's presidential inauguration in 1829. He was their guy. A mob of them descended on the White House with muddy boots and homemade clothes, destroying china, climbing on furniture. Lots got drunk on the presidential punch and punched staff and servants, sending the new president scurrying out of a side door for safety. As one attendee described it: "Ladies fainted, men were seen with bloody noses and such a scene of confusion took place as is impossible to describe."[4] The expanded electorate saw new parties and coalitions form when white men rushed in. The system preferred to absorb the changes rather than revoke the right and return to form.

Jackson's supporters splintered into two camps not long after he left the national stage: those for slavery and those against.[5] The question of Black people's place in democracy broke and reoriented the party system. It brought on civil war. It led to the assassination of a president: Abraham Lincoln was killed by Confederacy-conspiring actor John

Wilkes Booth, who became murderous after hearing Lincoln declare his support for Black men voting.

Once these new Black voters engaged, the victors changed. There was a redistribution of electoral power as formerly enslaved men arrived in Congress and state legislatures. Black people gathered up a couple reins to democracy, trying to manifest a people's destiny. These voters opposed enslavement, segregation, and racial oppression and inequality. Their stories were different. They challenged the nation's myths, pointing out hypocrisies and doublespeak. Many white Americans, either for political motives or ideological ones, banded with Black citizens and provided early glimpses of what a more equal multiracial democracy might look like. In some places, that proved too much, too disruptive to our myths and our understandings of who belongs. It would take less than ten years for the backlash to arrive, rolling back the specific right for which a president was killed. Violence was rarely far behind.

In Wilmington, North Carolina, a coalition of Black Republicans and white populists won the prominent local offices in the election of 1898. In pursuit of their economic interests, business leaders organized to break the multiracial coalition and, to do so, decided to stoke the racial conflicts with a long history in the state. It didn't take much effort. The result was the only successful coup d'état ever carried out on American soil. White supremacists mounted for action in search of a reason. They took inspiration from a state senator's remark that "there is but one chance and but one hope for the railroads to capture the next legislature, and that is for the nigger to be made the issue."[6] And so he was.

White supremacists—and this is not my attempt at labeling; they were self-avowed with a published manifesto—organized a mass media campaign and political connections to make the 1898 election a referendum on racial equality and its implications of interracial sex. One speech given by a white suffragist who opposed racial equality captured the cultural angle being weaponized: "If it needs lynching to protect woman's dearest possession from the ravening human beasts—then I say lynch, a thousand times a week if necessary."[7] For white populists in 1898, Black people winning office might not be that scary, but the suggestion that sex and babies with them come next did all the scaring necessary. When a Black writer responded to the speech, arguing that relationships between Black men and white women were happening and consensual, it was perceived as proof that the danger of miscegenation was real and underway. It was kindling for the fire that would race through the city as soon as the election results were in.

The racist campaign was so effective that when the multiracial coalition won the election, a violent horde assembled almost immediately to remove the newly elected by force and install a personally appointed government. The mob swept through the town and its Black neighborhoods, many dozens of people were killed, and Black and white coalition leaders were literally marched out of the city and threatened with death if they ever returned. The new self-installed local government wasted no time in welcoming the Jim Crow laws that would soon be found statewide and effectively remove Black people from the democracy.

Political violence seems to show up most often in places where, after years of rigid racial hierarchy, power begins to be shared more democratically among different racial or ethnic groups. Whether it's new voters changing election outcomes or a diverse coalition challenging those in power, the backlash is the same. And one has to wonder why that is. What about American democracy in the hands of people of color makes too many comfortable with the idea of over-throwing government, with undoing democracy altogether? Our democracy is treated as sacred only when it's in the hands of people like us; in the hands of others, it is a thing to be challenged, a thing to be avoided at great cost.

• • •

THAT CONVERSATION WITH JOHN about HBCUs comes to mind more often than it should. I've met lots of people like him over the years. They were in the military. Or neighbors. Or their kids played on the same soccer, basketball, and foot-ball teams as mine. They don't hate people because of their race or ethnicity. They do believe some stereotypes are well-earned. They acknowledge terrible things were done in the past but think the nation and its myths and its identity are generally good and worthy of admiration. What they really wish is that everyone would stop talking about race so much. Why can't we just all be Americans?

It's a rhetorical question but feels like a provocation. Because every time a new people begin acting like Americans—demanding access to democracy and leadership roles in it—they are made to slow down. And told that too much change too fast is not good. Patience. Wait your turn. But the new people keep pushing. Progress temporarily stalls when the backlash arrives, but they persist. And then, after decades of painstakingly slow advances, a Black family becomes the face of the nation. A Black-and-Indian woman with immigrant parents is telling the Founding Fathers' descendants what to do. And too many people like John feel as if the country they know is slipping away from them. They fear their destinies will soon be determined by different people, who may hold similar values but have a different way of life. And it becomes clearer that we can't all just be American because race gets in the way.

Not even the Huxtable ones will do.

Who's in charge seems to mean more to us than the system chosen to help select them. In 2016, the places most likely to redirect their votes to candidates with hard-line positions on race and ethnic issues were the predominantly white locales where the rate of racial change happened fastest.[8] New people rushing in changed things. Wherever it happens—in housing, schools, jobs, healthcare, wages, voting rights—people of color usually find they are perceived as threats to the traditionally American (read: white) way of life. Do you support housing equality if tomorrow all of your neighbors were immigrants from Central America? Do you support merit-only admissions for prestigious public high schools if 80 percent of the student body every year is Asian American in a place where they're just 10 percent of the population? Are you comfortable with the most important decisions affecting your life being made by Black people you didn't choose or vote for? Nothing challenges our commitment to democracy and the America of our myths more than shifting power imbalances among the racial groups.

The United States has a particular challenge. Those who question its commitment to democracy are met by an electorate that's more diverse than the founding generation could've imagined. Questions on our seriousness about racial equality have to explain how people of color are finding economic success and the ballot box in larger numbers than generations past. The United States is comfortable being multiracial. It is comfortable being democratic. But it is stressed to its limits when the color of democratic leadership begins to change. It's a status threat, fueling identity crises for the people and nation alike. And studies show that when the threat is couched as un-American, there's more tolerance for antidemocratic activities and more risk of political violence.[9] Our commitment to democracy isn't fraying so much as it is us having a hard time when new people lead it.

We're sore losers, seeing opponents at every turn and reacting poorly to big changes. Better to leave it all in the hands of classic heroes rather than newcomers.

But it will not be so. In 2020, for the third time in four presidential elections, a Black Democrat was on the winning ticket. Since Obama's election in 2008, the number of racial and ethnic minorities in Congress has nearly doubled, from just over 70 to almost 140. The Supreme Court is more diverse than it has ever been. Black mayors are leading the largest cities in the US as well as in red states such as Texas, Georgia, North Carolina, and Louisiana. Hispanic and Asian Americans are finding greater success in local and state politics, too.

Change is here. And the question is whether the classic participants of democracy will accept it when it no longer looks like them. Will it be legitimate in their eyes? Will white people love a democracy led by folks with different skin and histories and stories? Maybe it will all be too uncomfortable, unimaginable. Or worse, undesirable. For some, the thought of it all is just too much.

CHAPTER 4

Modeling Minorities

Andrew and Bobby hated each other. Or they were the best of friends. It's sometimes hard to tell with teenage boys. The constant ribbing and name-calling can be either masculine flexing or affection. Whatever the reason, I watched these two go at it every day in our physics class. Joke and laugh, debate and taunt, then get angry, argue, and insult. That's how it was with those two. But what may have begun as a couple of classmates yanking each other's chains turned into something different, ugly.

First, some background. Bobby's real name was not Bobby. I don't know what it was. He was a Japanese student, and like a number of other Asian American students, he took an American nickname so that other people didn't have to try to pronounce his birth name. Not every kid with an uncommon name did this. Of the ones that did, though, they were almost exclusively Asian. That was curious growing up in North Carolina at a time when elementary school teachers wheeled out big televisions on steel carts in the middle of the day to watch the Atlantic Coast Conference college basketball tournament. We could pronounce the name of Duke's former basketball coach—Krzyzewski—before we could tie our shoes.

It was also a time when Black folks' creativity with names reached new heights. And Ka'Taydreeyah wasn't shortening her name to Kate for anyone. But the kids from Vietnam and China and India and other places often didn't make us learn their names. They just went by Roger or Joanna or Ivy. Or Bobby.

And then there was Andrew. He checked all the boxes of being part of the in-crowd: varsity athlete, from a well-to-do family, a white guy serviceably attractive to the girls in his social circle, knew how to tell a good story. He would sometimes try on class clown for size, but the role never suited him. He was smart, affable. I met him the summer before senior year when he drove his car—an old beater he'd fixed up—off the road that ran behind my house. We heard the crash and ran out to make sure everyone was okay. This was before everyone had cell phones, so I invited him inside to call his parents. That autumn, we had two classes together and didn't even remember each other. We made the connection only after he wrote about the crash for a class assignment. It was hard to believe that Andrew—the dude who trash-talked Bobby daily—was the same kid in tears, calling his dad from my kitchen to report that he'd wrecked his summer project.

At the end of class each day, if the bickering wasn't going his way, Andrew would swing the two most hurtful words he could imagine at Bobby. *Hiroshima. Nagasaki.* Once he accompanied it with his hands slowly spreading out in an exploding motion as he whispered, "Boom."

Atomic bombs are nothing to joke about, especially not to someone from the only nation to be hit with one. Bobby's response to the nuclear heckling was always silence. There was no retort or rebuttal, no one-upmanship. Most kids just thought he was afraid. I thought it was the other way around—Andrew felt threatened by Bobby. It was a time when Americans feared Japan's economy would become stronger than ours. We were falling behind Asian nations in science and engineering. We wanted the cars they made instead of our own. All of that was packed in Andrew's animus. And it was the early years of the model minority myth.

Across the hallway from physics was French class. Annie sat behind me. That wasn't her given name. She was Taiwanese; Annie was her American name. We struck up a natural friendship and joked daily in class. We were the only two people of color in the class, but I don't think Annie and I talked about race or racism once. For a while she was my only Asian friend. I knew, and learned to pronounce almost perfectly, her real name.

After losing touch, Annie and I briefly reconnected on social media about a decade ago. We traded updates on life's twists and turns. A few months later, her dad was beaten mercilessly while out for a walk. They never caught who did it. The police said it was a hate crime. Annie was heartbroken but resolved to take action. She used social media to try and find her father's assailant and also to spread awareness of anti-Asian violence. For all her and her family did to fit in, racism still found them.

I remember thinking that if this was how the model minority was treated, what hope did other people of color have? The American Dream. Model behavior. Trying to fit in. None of it means you will be welcomed or accepted. And there's nothing you can do about it.

• • •

WHEN RESEARCHERS TALK WITH ASIAN AMERICANS, they find that many of them understand *American* to mean *white*. In an effort to fit in, they have sometimes adopted white-sounding names and wished for the fairer skin, blond hair, and blue eyes.[1] In the United States, being a different race or ethnicity sometimes feels like you are inescapably less American. Skin color and features give you away no matter how much you subscribe to the American way of life.

The model minority label suggests that a particular race or ethnicity possesses qualities held in high esteem but that they are not traditionally American. Which is to say, white. Its origins date back nearly a century. The historian Ellen Wu describes the characterization of Asian Americans and immigrants—specifically from Japan and China—in the 1940s and 1950s as being marked as *definitively not white*. Discrimination against Asians permeated every facet of American life, from work and housing to immigration and citizenship. Then, according to Wu, as the geopolitical interests of the nation evolved after World War II and the Civil Rights Movement took center stage domestically, a new narrative emerged. They were now "the model minority—a racial group distinct from the white majority, but lauded as well assimilated, upwardly mobile, politically nonthreatening, and *definitively not Black*."[2]

White politicians in the late 1960s seized on the term *model minority* and used it in one of two ways.[3] The first was to point to Asian Americans as proof that through hard work and assimilation, anyone could make it in the United States. Politicians' motivations here were to get government out of the racism business following a set of violent and contentious years at the close of the Civil Rights Movement. If there was proof that a group historically discriminated against had risen to the highest of heights, then, the argument went, the government had clearly done its part in leveling the playing field. The second was to weaponize Asian Americans as a counterexample to Black people specifically, discrediting claims from activists and movement leaders that the United

States was a racist nation. The more the model minority concept stuck, the more credence was given to the idea that Black people's problems were a cultural product of being too lazy, too unintelligent, too impulsive.

Altogether, the model minority concept is a political one meant to preserve, rather than upend, racial hierarchies and disparities. It is usually defined as the idea that "Asian Americans are more academically and economically successful in society compared to other racial minorities due to their supposedly stronger values of hard work and determination."[4] And psychologists have found when Asian Americans internalize the model minority myth—that is, when they buy into the idea that they're an exceptional people who are particularly suited to excel in the United States—they are more likely to believe in a colorblind society and to oppose affirmative action.[5] And to hold anti-Black attitudes.

Studies show that Asian people who strive to acculturate to white America often adopt negative views of Black people. Moreover, those who internalize the model minority concept are also more likely to struggle with Asian identity markers—like wanting to change names and appearance—and with judging their fellow group members based on how closely they mirror the white standard. And how well they avoid the Black one.

The model minority concept is a game of opposites, pitting Asian and Black Americans against each other and stuffing other people of color in between. But whereas Black

Americans are told they can be an exceptional minority *person* who climbs the ladder, the myth tells us that Asian Americans are an exceptional minority *people*. Taking new names, like Bobby and Annie, is seen as proof of cultural assimilation. They are the actions of a people seeking belonging. Unlike Ka'Taydreeyah, the myth goes, who insists on being different.

ERICA KIM WANTED TO BE a Girl Scout. She was in Northern Virginia, in elementary school. Her parents, who'd both immigrated from South Korea, contacted the school's troop but were told it was full and not taking new members. The family was disappointed, naturally. They recognized the importance that civic institutions play in becoming part of a community. But they accepted that Erica would have to wait her turn.

Then what often happens in the United States happened. Her mom noticed that new students were being welcomed into the troop, and they all had one thing in common: they were white girls. The realization that the troop rejected Erica because she was Asian painfully set in. So she raised some hell. "I was too young to know what was going on," Erica told me recently. "But I knew something wasn't right." Because of her mother's fierce challenge, the troop let Erica join very briefly just before her father's job carried the family to California. "That was the first memory I have of my mother advocating for me because of something race-related," she said. And then, with her eyes skyward, as if trying to recall the feeling of this next moment, she sighed. "That is the first memory I have of being aware that I was Asian." Erica, a little girl born in the American South, learned that people thought she was more than just different. They considered her foreign.

In the 1970s, South Korea was led by a former military general who championed what he called *Korean-style democracy*—an authoritarian dictatorship that focused on the economy, undertook massive infrastructure projects, and suppressed political opposition. Before its president was assassinated, the promise of opportunity led Erica's mother and family to the United States when her mom was just twelve years old. Her father made the same choice a few years later. The two met in Southern California and began a family, and her father soon moved into Christian ministry. Erica is one of four children, and she was born in Kentucky, where her father was attending seminary. The family pinballed the country as he moved churches, which meant that Erica spent kindergarten through high school in California and different parts of Virginia.

The Kims' cultural approach to life in the United States reflected the household's regional duality, alternating locations on the East and West Coasts. Both English and Korean were spoken in the home, and the dinner table reflected the shared cultures: "My mom would make Korean food a couple nights," Erica said, "and then, like, it's your lasagna and your taco nights." Though their schools were often predominantly white, they attended Korean churches, which were where they maintained a cultural connection to their family and ancestral land.

Back in Virginia for middle school, Erica was one of only two Asian American students in a place that was almost entirely comprised of white and Black people. Intolerance and adolescent posturing combined to make her days long. Erica told me matter-of-factly, "I don't think it was ever physical bullying, just the standard things like 'Go back to your country!' and stuff about being Chinese."

• • •

THE QUEST TO BELONG IS quintessentially human. And it is harder in diverse democratic societies. The nation's size and large multiethnic population mean American teens, high on energy and low on experience, begin a particular cultural identity journey shaped by the groups they want to belong to, the ones they can belong to, and the ones they want to avoid. The resulting jockeying for position has social impacts, and race is an extremely powerful force.

When children of color are told they do not—and perhaps cannot—belong in the United States, it changes their relationship with the country. Slowly, being American feels like a goal they can strive toward but never fully attain. Different groups, based on their histories and attributes, have devised different strategies to overcome the barriers to their belonging. Erica's experience in school is typical for many immigrant families, especially Asian ones. Her parents wanted to create a sense of belonging for their children in the communities where they lived and in the nation where they were citizens. But there was no avoiding the reality that being ethnically Korean meant that there would always be people who made it harder for them to feel like they belonged here.

When people are asked about Americanness with race removed from the question, research from sociologists and psychologists finds "strong consensus about the defining characteristics of the American identity across ethnic groups,"[6] as one set of scholars puts it. That is, we all pretty much agree on what it means to be American and who can be one. Yet when a diverse group of people is individually asked about how "American" different races and ethnicities are—or which group most personifies the national identity—white people are identified as the most American group. The group said to be the least? Asian Americans.

Other studies show that when groups are compared directly—for example, who is more American? Black people or Asian people?—a hierarchy comes into view. White people rank themselves first, followed by Asian people, and then Black people. Asian Americans generally consider themselves just as American as Black people and less than white people. But Black folks think of themselves as more American than Asian people and as running neck and neck with white people.

No matter one's race, ethnicity, or name, experiencing discrimination and being told that you're less American have real effects on a person's sense of connection to others. Belonging is an intrinsic need to form bonds with other people that are reinforced through frequent positive interactions.[7] People feel like they belong when they have constructive relationships and personal agency. The opposite is to feel ignored, excluded, or ambivalent about acceptance and connection. Asian and Black Americans were the two groups with the lowest levels of national belonging, with just one in four feeling connected to and accepted in the United States. And Asian Americans had the highest rate of feeling excluded. No group feels less local belonging than Asian Americans, and no one feels it more locally than Black Americans.[8] It's no coincidence that though segregation remains high, Asian Americans are the least segregated and Black folks are the most.[9]

Erica's childhood is a testimony to how earnestness of effort may never be sufficient to be accepted. At eight years old, she learned that people thought of her differently because of her race, when all she wanted to do was be a Brownie in the Girl Scouts. The many experiences that followed—and the unavoidable encounters with the model minority myth—caused an adolescent Erica to actively work to defy stereotypes and be perceived as the "cool Asian." By the time she showed up in my graduate school classroom over a decade later, she was grappling with how one embraces their ethnic difference from the prototypical Americans while also wanting to belong. To help make sense of it all, one of the places she turned to was the Black American experience.

TRAGEDY STRUCK WHEN ERICA WAS in high school. During her sophomore year, her father became ill. And the next year, he passed away. Not only did the loss of her father devastate the family, but it also put them in dire financial straits.

One of the ways she managed the grieving process was to throw herself into her schoolwork. Socially, many of her friends were white, but the family was living in a part of Northern Virginia that had a relatively sizable Asian American population. As such, she became adept at traversing different worlds, straddling lines of class, race, ethnicity, and region. When she was a high school senior, she was pining for something different. She wanted to meet new people, to have new experiences. She decided to go out of state for college and was admitted, with a generous aid package, to an elite university in the South. A godsend.

We all leave high school different from when we entered, but losing a parent along the way means identity journeys and questions about life's purpose can arrive with a sudden urgency and intensity.

In college, for the first time in her life, Erica leaned deeply into her Asian American identity. "Race was something that I was only beginning to really explore in college," Erica told me. "I ended up having a lot of Asian American friends—mostly Chinese and Taiwanese. Not so much other Korean students, which is a whole other conversation. But having a social group that was heavily Asian American or East Asian American allowed me to explore other parts of me." Those friendships helped her navigate university life and cope with ethnic slights. Like a professor recording the wrong grade after confusing her with the other Asian girl in class. Later, though Erica has lived her entire life in the United States and majored in English, people would sometimes remark, with surprise, "Your English is so good!"

She calls herself Asian American rather than Korean American for reasons that feel familiar to me as a Black person. Having friends from across East Asia helped her touch the corners of an ethnic solidarity that African Americans have long practiced. Such solidarities can sometimes reinforce the same stereotypes that broader society holds. Erica notes that Asian women are often judged on how thin, feminine, deferential, and fair-skinned they are. She also points out that ethnic authenticity is policed. Because she's never been to South Korea and isn't fluent in the language, some of the other Korean students were reluctant to engage with and accept her. When a Black person is accused of "acting white," other Black folks label them an *Oreo*—black on the outside, white on the inside. For East Asian people, the insult from other group members is *Twinkie*—white on the inside and yellow on the outside.

Erica completed her education without ever being taught the history of Asian people in the United States. She took a staff job at a private university in Washington, DC, while also mentoring low-income, first-generation undergraduate students in a scholarship program. She visited the National Museum of African American History and Culture. It was a moving—and frustrating—experience. "I was so overwhelmed by the amount of information," she said, shaking her head a little. "And how much of that I had not known."

She couldn't help but wonder about all the stories to be told of the Asian experience. It came to a head one afternoon while out with family friends. She recalled passing a statue and saying, "It'd be nice if there were some statues of Asian Americans." One of them replied, "So who would you want?" She could only think of celebrities. That bothered her. Soon, at the recommendation of her colleague, she was in my graduate seminar on Black America and public policy. She was an exceptional student, thoughtful and compassionate and curious. The next spring Erica appeared in my classroom bearing good news. She was headed to an Ivy for a master's degree to examine questions of racial equity in education.

. . .

IN THE SUMMER OF 2023, the Supreme Court finally did what many feared it would do for decades. Affirmative action in college admissions was effectively killed. The justices had been weighing in on race-based preferences for college admissions for some time. The 1978 decision in *Regents of the University of California v. Bakke* struck down racial quotas but stipulated that race could be one of many factors in admissions decisions. In ensuing cases, the use of race as a factor in admissions decisions was generally upheld. The plaintiffs were always white. Until the conservative activist behind previous failed attempts to have racial preferences ruled unconstitutional decided to bring a suit featuring model minorities. The admissions policies at Harvard and the University of North Carolina at Chapel Hill were the targets, brought on behalf of Asian American applicants who argued they were passed over for less qualified Black, Hispanic, and white candidates. In 2023's *Students for Fair Admissions v. Harvard* and *Students for Fair Admissions v. University of North Carolina*, the model minority myth was used for the ammunition to bring about affirmative action's demise.

The issue is local, too. The best high school in the country is up the road from my house, and students of Asian ethnicity are incredibly overrepresented. The county is home to more than a million people: 47 percent of them are white, 20 percent are Asian, 17 percent Hispanic, and 10 percent Black. In this school of nearly two thousand students who made it through an extremely competitive admissions process, 72 percent are Asian, 18 percent white, and Hispanic and Black students make up just 5 percent of the student body.

It's out of balance, sure. But restricting admissions numbers of racial and ethnic groups based on each's share of the overall population is just a quota by another name. Set no limits, though, and a question arises: How much out of balance is too much? And how few of a group is too few? Communities with substantial Asian American populations are grappling with these questions. The school board wanted a more representative student body, so it revised the decision process to help more non-Asian students gain admission. Afterward, the number of Black and Hispanic admitted students quadrupled to just over 18 percent, and admitted Asian students decreased from nearly three-quarters of new students to just over half.[10] Naturally, local Black parents and civil rights organizations supported the changes while many Asian parents and advocacy groups opposed it. A federal court got involved, and it ruled that the new process could stand.

The school board in San Francisco pursued a similar

strategy of tinkering with the admissions process to the city's most prestigious high school to reduce the high percentage of Asian American students and fill those slots with more Black and Hispanic students.[11] While relatively few Asian Americans voted in the school board election, they turned out en masse when a recall vote was scheduled. Chinese Americans led a successful effort to remove three school board members—one Mexican woman, one Samoan man, and one Black woman who'd once gone on an anti-Asian tirade on social media, invoking "the 'model minority' BS" and white supremacy and saying Asian Americans were acting like the new "house n****r."[12]

The end of affirmative action in education was always likely to come at the hands of the model minority myth. Pitting racial and ethnic groups—real or imagined—against one another is a tried-and-true tactic that people have employed for as long as humans have engaged in conflict. It works more than it should. It's also destructive. Manufacturing competition and tension among racial groups soon takes on a life of its own. Violence is almost always a byproduct.

• • •

WHEN THE CORONAVIRUS SHUT DOWN the world in March 2020, it wasn't long before Asian Americans were targeted with racism and xenophobia and violence. The Trump administration, conservative media, and many of Trump's followers started calling the disease *kung flu* and the *Chinese*, or *Wuhan*, *virus*. Not very subtle. Reported hate crimes against Asian people skyrocketed, more than tripling in 2021 from the previous year.[13] And those are just the reported cases. Many go unreported because of language barriers, shame, and distrust of authority.

Some of these crimes were caught on camera and played over and over again in the media. And some of them were committed by people of color. The one I can't shake is the viral video of a hulking Black man punching a sixty-seven-year-old Filipina more than a hundred times outside of a building elevator. He was sentenced to over seventeen years in prison. This became a theme for conservative media, hoping to distract from the president's increasingly intolerant language. In New York City, local politicians used videos of Black people assaulting Asian people to paint their opponents as weak on crime—despite the fact that three-quarters of anti-Asian hate crimes committed during Covid were committed by white people.[14] Asian Americans across the country were living with a new fear.

Like Erica. I asked her what life had been like for her during Covid.

"I very much felt the fear of going out in public, even going down from my apartment to the pizza shop right on my block. I didn't know if I would get my head slammed against a concrete wall or be shoved down a flight of stairs." She let out a deep, emotional sigh. "It got really severe and really scary. I had to stop listening to the stories because it just felt really scary. And though I know I'm 'inherently equal,' is my life equally valued? Absolutely not."

We didn't avoid the hard stuff. I asked what she made of the videos of Black men assaulting Asian women.

"I think a lot of Asian Americans, including myself, wondered if it would be wrong to publicize something that happened to an Asian person if the perpetrator were a Black man especially. Because we—some of us don't want to feed this narrative that Black men are violent or perpetrators of crimes. But I'll add one other thing: I think there were some of us, the ones who think a lot about race and their own lived experience, who wanted some sort of signal or something from a lot of their Black friends and didn't get it."

I was certainly guilty.

Erica hoped for the same thing I did. That the deadly virus might present an opportunity for a national multi-racial solidarity to emerge. That we would bind together to defeat this threat to our individual and collective well-being. When the issue became racialized and politicized, we'd both hoped that at least people of color would rally around one another. When neither happened at the scale we thought it might have, it was disappointing.

During Erica's senior year of college, two East Asian friends pledged Alpha Kappa Alpha, the first historically Black sorority. She and a few other friends attended a new member presentation for them, and it left an impression.

"I remember watching this very-late-at-night ceremony and finding it so intriguing," she told me. "It was an incredibly tight community and sisterhood. When it was over and we were leaving, I remember saying, 'I didn't know that that pocket of the school existed.'" It was another way of saying two things. One, that given her life experience, she didn't know about the cultural practices of historically Black fraternities and sororities or that they were playing out on campus. And two, that there were places where interracial solidarity among Asian and Black people her age was not a foreign concept, where one was readily welcomed into community with the other.

As Erica and I wrapped up our conversation, I could see tears beginning to form in her eyes. "Thank you so much for this. It was really good for me to think through this out loud and in the moment without filtering my answers. It felt safe. Being able to share some of my thoughts . . ." Her voice quivered. "I'm getting emotional because it really does mean a lot to me. To have my experiences seen and heard is really meaningful."

• • •

THE MYTH OF THE MODEL MINORITY poses a haunting question: *What if it's right?*

What if the reason Asian Americans have outsize success today is because they've done a better job of solving the riddle of socioeconomic mobility in America? The median household wealth for Asian Americans is the highest.[15] They have the highest median income, the highest home ownership rate among people of color and the highest college participation rates, and they own 11 percent of the nation's small businesses despite being just 7 percent of the population.[16] What would have to happen in the United States for Black people to hit these same marks? I understand why we haven't. But I don't understand why Asian Americans have. The model minority myth provides a ready answer.

That answer, though, is wrong. At best, it's incomplete. It misses the growing inequality among Asian Americans. Poverty levels are high among some groups. Educational attainment is below average among others. Incarceration rates are uneven. The myth makes it seem like every ethnicity from the Asian continent that makes it to the United States has mastered the climb to the American Dream. It's just not true. Much of the group's prosperity is driven by Indian and Taiwanese Americans. They have household incomes twice as high as the Asian groups at the bottom, like Laotians and Cambodians, and are four times more likely to have college degrees. And yet Laotians have a third more household income than Black people.

So, what if it's right? What if it's primarily Black people's fault that we've not kept pace with the mythical model minority? What might the path look like for us to close the gap between us and the rest of America? It's not just the result of ingenuity and hard work, neither of which has ever been enough to ensure our safety and shared prosperity.

The project of belonging in the United States today is a difficult one. Race precedes us all. And we've not yet settled the matter of what it is we will belong to. Who the nation will be tomorrow is an open question.

But chances are that the nation will long be thought of as a white one. And that will come with demands, large and small. It's a demand that the rest of us must assimilate to improve our chances of making it in America. Sometimes we bend ourselves. Play the game. Wear the mask. We will even change our names to be accepted.

Until we won't.

CHAPTER 5

Sound of the Police

During my last week in the military—a career that lingered twenty years despite my plan for it to be a job that lasted four—a fellow officer pointed at the flat-screen televisions mounted on the wall of a classified conference room inside the Pentagon. There are TVs everywhere in this famous five-sided building that sits on land confiscated during the Civil War from the estate of Confederate general Robert E. Lee. As soon as you step into a meeting space or operations center from somewhere along the building's seventeen miles of hallway, you're greeted by the colorful chyrons of cable news, often on a wall of televisions teeming with telegenic anchors. In the classified places, some of the monitors display secret information, like the locations of a nation's ships or a surveillance feed from somewhere on Earth. But all the others are tuned to cable news, serving as a window to the outside world in rooms where actual windows are forbidden. All the expected players are there. CNN. Fox News. MSNBC. CNBC. And so on. My colleague was windshield-wiping his arm at the screens as a way of pointing at all of them, and he asked, "What do you think about that?"

He didn't need to be precise about which channel and which thing he was talking about—most of the news seemed to be on the same topic: football and the flag. I looked up to see segments about Colin Kaepernick, the quarterback for the San Francisco 49ers at the time. He'd kneeled during the national anthem, the televisions' closed-captioning sputtering out blocks of text with his rationale. It was the summer of 2016. We were a nation with a Black president and naïve enough to believe that Donald Trump couldn't actually win the presidential election. The summer of 2016 was hot, leading to one of the warmest years in recorded history. And racial tensions seemed to follow suit. The season was filled with more than a hundred Black Lives Matter protests in several dozen cities following the police killings of Alton Sterling in Baton Rouge and Philando Castile in Minnesota. Video from both fatal encounters appeared everywhere. Bystanders caught Sterling's killing on their cell phones. Castile's girlfriend, wanting to ensure the world knew of his unjust death, began live-streaming the scene from inside the car . . . Castile bleeding out in the driver's seat while his girlfriend's four-year-old daughter screamed for her mother's life to be spared.

Kaepernick explained that his protest was designed to call attention to racial injustice, including the brutal policing of Black people.

Not wanting to have this conversation at work just days before retirement, I shrugged, demurring with a question, "Freedom of speech, right?"

Thankfully, the officer, a white air force guy from Colorado, pressed me, a Black sailor from North Carolina, on the issue. "I've served with you, saluted alongside you—I know how you feel about the flag. But do you think the police treat Black people differently?"

There was no shrugging off this question.

JUST BEFORE THE START OF my military career two decades earlier, I was out smoking cigars with friends. That sounds more sophisticated an outing than it actually was. Here's a more accurate one: we got some Black & Milds.

We got a pack of Black & Mild—five inside, each pipe tobacco wrapped in chocolate-colored paper with a plastic tip—and we smoked 'em. Standing around my car, hanging and philosophizing. My boys and I had gotten together to celebrate my imminent departure for military training, and now it was the part of the night when we choose to linger rather than say goodbye. In these circles, goodbyes are said in the subtleties. In the lingering. That night we held court until the plastic tips warmed our fingers.

On my drive home in the wee hours that morning on an isolated stretch of interstate, reflections of blue lights lit up the car's interior. I had that feeling. Within minutes I stood handcuffed as one policeman ransacked my car and the other informed me that one of my headlights was out. And then, adding matter-of-factly the real reason for the stop, "Besides, we saw you smoking that blunt." He'd assumed the Black & Mild that I was holding was actually a cigar covertly stuffed with marijuana. By the end of the ordeal, I was stuffed into the back seat of a police cruiser on my way to jail, arrested—not for the headlight or the pipe tobacco wisping in the ashtray but because, as an absent-minded college student, I'd forgotten to renew my license after it had expired several weeks earlier.

In that jail, I was scared to death. Alone in a cell. As I waited to be released to my father, another person was thrown in. I'll never forget his face. He was like a movie character: the aging dreadlocked brother wearing a red, black, and green crochet kufi from a Spike Lee joint, smelling of incense or getting roughed up by the cops. And suddenly, unfolding a couple feet from me, was a scene that felt more familiar than it should. It was all there—the Black man, the long dreads, the massive hematoma on his fore-head that trailed blood down his face and pooled onto the concrete floor where he lay.

The next month I put on a military uniform and promised to die for America.

• • •

THESE BOOKENDS TO MY MILITARY SERVICE took on more meaning in the spring of 2020. Covid was on the scene, making an American public mostly captive to their homes just as the names George Floyd, Ahmaud Arbery, and Breonna Taylor made national news. There was round-the-clock coverage of peaceful protests and violent unrest following the release of video and audio capturing the vigilante murder of Arbery and the police killings of Floyd and Taylor. Floyd's murder struck such a chord that much of the nation risked their health during the pandemic to gather and protest.

Calls for justice rang from all corners. The calls turned into action, and demonstrations decrying the police's treatment of Black people soon followed. Some of the protests lingered too long or splintered. Riots broke out. Looting happened. Visuals of violent confrontations with heavily armed police forces filled screens and pages. Though the vast majority of protests were civil exercises of the First Amendment rights to assemble peaceably and to speak freely about the effects of racism on our liberty and society, the nation was on edge.

The country did not feel at peace because it wasn't.

And the tension became its own spectacle. The brew of militarized police, enraged citizens, and criminal looters—bursting into scenes of chaos backlit by burning cars and flash-bangs—was a powerful elixir. Dramatic images and impassioned appeals to stop the violence flooded traditional and social media outlets, broadcasting the destruction and airing competing ideas about how to restore order.

Political leaders at all levels of government took their cases to the public, typically sorting themselves into one of two ideological camps. Keisha Lance Bottoms, who was Atlanta's mayor, characterized one side, telling her city in an emotional speech that breaking windows and looting stores run counter to the spirit of the protests and detract from their calls for racial justice. Most of the country wasn't supposed to hear it like she said it. "You're not protesting anything running out with brown liquor in your hands and breaking windows in this city," she said. "If you want change in America, go and register to vote! . . . You are disgracing our city, you are disgracing the life of George Floyd and every other person who has been killed in this country. We are better than this! We're better than this as a city, we are better than this as a country. Go home. Go home!"[1]

The then-president Trump characterized the other side, which suggested that the riots weren't a symptom of a larger national problem; the rioters were the problem. And that problem required a response of overwhelming force. Trump sent federal agents with nonlethal munitions and smoke canisters to surge against peaceful White House demonstrators. He had them clear a path so he could cross the street with the senior-most military officer in tow for a photo op in front a damaged historic church. There, he held the Bible upside down.

Predictably, when racial tensions reach fever pitch, both sides make appeals to the patron saint, the Rev. Dr. Martin Luther King Jr. In explaining the anger that boils over into destruction, we are reminded of his statement from a 1967 speech at Stanford University: "A riot is the language of the unheard."[2] Others note that the principal order of business should be to restore order, echoing another King quote from the exact same speech: "I will always continue to say that riots are socially destructive and self-defeating."[3]

As the protests continued across the country, we risked getting tripped up, once again, on arguments about *how* people protest rather than *why*. The destruction of property becomes more concerning than human rights violations. Yet even our myths tell us this is wrong. Nearly 250 years after Massachusetts colonists destroyed private property by dumping the contents of a British East India Company shipment into the Boston Harbor, no one gives a damn about the tea. But the principle inspiring that protest—"No taxation without representation"—lives on. The nation's capital, still a Black city, wears this badge of protest on its license plates.

There was a chance that Floyd's murder would compel the country to be better, a little more perfect. And when such a chance presents itself, we are duty bound to grapple with an abiding sense of injustice—felt acutely in Black America—that has long been at the root of the nation's biggest and most enduring challenge.

THE NIGHT THE POLICE STOPPED ME for smoking a Black & Mild, all three of us—the two white officers and me—became part of a larger narrative about the relationship between Black people and policing. Each encounter brings a set of stories and experiences with it. James Baldwin observed that history shapes our present, is bound up inside us, and influences our lives in ways that we do not always understand. History does not absolve us of the consequences of our personal behavior, but it does provide context for the choices we make, our interactions with one another, and our worldviews.

For Black people in particular, the murders of George Floyd, Ahmaud Arbery, and Breonna Taylor are not aberrations in an otherwise fair and just America. Rather, they are wholly consistent with the history of policing and vigilantism experienced since the nation's inception, knowledge of which has been passed through the generations as cautionary tales. Each incident between an unarmed Black person and law enforcement or self-appointed watchmen reminds us of a people's wisdom. It's impossible to understand the protests in the summer of 2020, peaceful and otherwise, without a fuller appreciation of this history.

• • •

THE CREATION OF THE BLACK AMERICAN occurred in a system that rewarded the taking of a Black person's liberty and exacted harsh penalties when the racial order was breached. Violence was used at every point of enslavement, becoming the primary language in which the nation spoke to these new Americans. As enslaved people sought freedom from bondage, marshalling the same spirit that inspired a young nation to declare its independence in the summer of 1776, slave patrols were established to deter uprisings, to capture those who dared to escape, and to enforce the laws and codes that further stripped Black Americans of their autonomy. State-sanctioned brutality—carried out by private citizens, commissioned patrols, and state militias—was the means to keep Black people down, delivering a bastardized idea of justice such that any reason, or no reason at all, was enough for it to be employed with impunity.

After the United States' victory over the Confederacy, enslavement was made unconstitutional. And the formerly enslaved became citizens. And formerly enslaved Black men gained the right to vote. And in very short order, localities, states, and the Union shifted. The racial hierarchy had not been dismantled but critically fractured. This interruption of the racial order—enforced with federal troops—brought backlash. The vigilantism of white segregationists became the primary vehicle for depriving the newly freed men and women of their rights. Attempts by Black victims to bring their white assailants to justice only bore more strange fruit.

Over a half century after the Emancipation Proclamation, physical violence and economic oppression in the South pushed millions of Black Americans north and west in search of work and security. They may have left the rank vigilantism experienced in the South, but they were soon met by overpolicing in their new cities. The arrival of so many Black people in a relatively short period of time altered local politics and increased economic competition with working-class, indigent, and immigrant white residents. Law enforcement became the means by which the local racial order—animated by casting Black people as economic, political, and social threats—was established and managed.

White European immigrants, also seeking stability, were treated as second-class citizens but were awarded patronage jobs that empowered them to control the more undesirable Black arrivals. A significant share of police officers across the North and Midwest consisted of European immigrants. Studies of the early twentieth century show that arrests and incarceration rates of Black people increased along with the proportion of police who were white immigrants.[4] As many Black newspapers chronicled at the time, police harassment, raids, and brutality in Black communities were commonplace. The urgent pleas of Black Americans for accountability and redress went largely ignored by political and institutional leaders.

The stories from early- and mid-twentieth-century America are legion. Isaac Woodard, a Black World War II veteran fresh from the Pacific, had his eyes gouged out by police in Batesburg, South Carolina. Claude Neal was lynched—a mob of a hundred white vigilantes shot, hanged, burned, and castrated him, taking fingers and toes for souvenirs. And these weren't distinct occurrences—police and mobs often collaborated in extrajudicial acts of violence. A 1933 study published in the book *The Tragedy of Lynching* estimated that police officers participated in at least half of lynchings, and either condoned or turned a blind eye to nearly all the others.

Nonviolent civil-rights activists were often met with police and posse violence. Black Americans were subjected to beatings, lynchings, bombings, and shootings that rarely resulted in justice for the victims. Images of peaceful Black protesters in the clutches of lunging German shepherds, clubbed by uniformed police, and shielding one another from water-cannon blasts are seared into the American psyche.

The lessons of this history have been painfully clear to each successive generation of Black Americans: policing by agents of the state—as well as by private citizens—is accompanied by an ever-present risk of violence, perpetrators of the violence often go unpunished, and Black citizens' accounts of the violence are often tossed aside. Altogether, even as the nation made lasting strides in extending the rights and privileges of citizenship to Black people, the ability to receive justice when wronged by agents of the state or other citizens was a right that remained out of their reach.

So when Ahmaud Arbery was accosted by murderous vigilantes while jogging through his neighborhood, Black people remembered Trayvon Martin's killing by an overzealous neighborhood watchman. We remembered the 1955 lynching of fourteen-year-old Emmett Till. And when George Floyd died as a police officer kneeled on his neck or Tyre Nichols was tased and beaten to death by the police, Black America remembered the stories of similarly brutal policing over the years: policemen blinding Isaac Woodard in an alleyway, choking out Eric Garner on a street in Staten Island, shooting Walter Scott in the back in an empty North Charleston lot—the list goes on.

. . .

IT'S NOT HARD TO CONNECT the dots of the narrative that emerges from this history. There's no need to force a story where there isn't one or identify patterns that aren't there. The history and the continued incidents manifest as a clear articulation of the long-standing adverse relationship between the state and its Black citizens. It's characterized by mistrust, conflict, and the sense that law enforcement is free of oversight and consequence when engaging Black people. This conception is in the ether—few Black folks can remember the exact day it dawned on them that policing was going to be different for them.

Back on the side of that interstate as a college kid pulled over late into the night—one policeman at my window and the other lurking over my right shoulder on the car's passenger side with a flashlight in one hand and a holster palmed in the other—I can tell you that the fear racing through me was a product of this sordid history. I grew up the child of college-educated professional parents in a white Southern subdivision, where police were implicitly trusted and rarely seen. My view of police was informed not so much by personal experience as by cultural proverb. Issued along with my driver's license came parental guidance for any interaction with police: *Survive the encounter; worry about your rights and liberty later.* The bleeding brother on the floor of my cell confirmed the wisdom in that counsel.

Many moons later, when my son was in preschool, we were driving one night from Maryland to my hometown in North Carolina. I was on the interstate, speeding. Doing almost eighty in a sixty-five-mile-per-hour-speed-limit zone. The cop was sitting slick—I didn't see him at all. His headlights suddenly popped up behind me, followed almost immediately by the ominous blue-and-white swirls of light. I knew the routine: give the policeman my military identification and, in a separate gesture, hand over my license and insurance. I could tell it worked by how his demeanor changed.

He went back to his car to run my information. I looked in my back seat. My four-year-old son was silently in tears. Scared to death. We do not trash police in our house. And we had not exposed our preschool-age children to the ugly realities of racist violence. But somewhere, four years into life as a Black boy, a fear of the police had found him.

The racial tensions at play between Black citizens and law enforcement are emblematic of a bigger question about the powers of the state and the liberty of its people. Racial inequality has long been the primary issue that exposes the gap between what the United States says it is and what it does. Slavery is often referred to as America's original sin not because of white people's treatment of Black people but because a nation founded on the high-minded ideals of liberty and equality allowed the enslavement of human beings to persist. That contradiction, and all the constitutional rights violations that followed, is not an unfortunate relic of history; it is a lethal paradox that threatens the nation's identity. And when a nation experiences a deep identity crisis, political violence follows. Some of its people destroy neighborhood blocks. Some of its people riot at the Capitol.

The protests in response to the killing of George Floyd were not just expressions of outrage at his death or at the long history of the use of excessive force in Black communities. They were also a people's rejection of the state's use of violence as a response to hard problems. They were a demonstration against the government's infringement of the people's rights, liberties, and autonomy.

The rallying cry *Black Lives Matter* evolved into an assertion that, given our nation's history on race, America can realize its potential only if it recognizes the inherent value of a group it once enslaved, and accepts that group's authority to hold the state and its agents accountable.

AT THEIR CORE, BLACK FOLKS' historical responses to abuses of power by law enforcement are really a test of a foundational American principle: if we are a nation in which government derives its power from the consent of the governed, then the ability to keep that power in check rests with the people. But if a people, because of little more than their race, has been excluded from the right to hold the state accountable for its actions or inaction, then the foundation of the nation's liberal democracy is faulty. The United States is only as good as it is to whichever peoples it considers the "least of these."

The summer-of-2020 protests were not simply about race relations. They were not about whether white and Black people should get along better or like each other more. They were affirmations of the need for reckoning, for an answer to the question of why race remains a distinctly divisive issue capable of exposing the gap between the nation's ideals and its actions.

That summer's protests were different. They were more intense, widespread, sustained, and focused than previous recent responses to police and vigilante violence against unarmed Black people. Protests took place in every state in the country, and the participants were Americans of every race, ethnicity, sex, age, and religion. If there was an epiphany, it was the same for twenty-first-century Americans as it was for those in previous centuries: We are people who do not take kindly to unjust and unwarranted government intrusions on our lives or opportunities. If there was a chance for this time to be different, the new wrinkle needed to be that many more Americans of all kinds understand that other people's liberty is essential to our own.

The summer of 2020 was just the latest chapter in a more consequential tale. It's more expedient to reduce conflicts between the state and its people to be interpersonal prejudices run amok, blaming it on people simply not getting along. Any attempts to consider the broader role that race plays usually devolve into debates about whether racism is a good explanation, a convenient scapegoat, or a magical and malleable fiction. The easy, but incorrect, explanation is that individual behavior was the only culprit. That some folks just didn't know how to act. In this telling, the arguments are always about America's rotten fruit—bad apples in the police force, bad apples among the protesters, bad apples among the people and politicians.

But the truth is that racism is a unique and painful reminder of how the nation has historically fallen short and of those shortfalls' lingering effects. It's a scathing critique of the use of state power to deny the very thing our nation was created to establish: a government based on the equality of citizens and on the protection of their liberty. It spotlights the misalignment among our principles, our mythology, and our practices.

To put a finer point on it: the persistence of racial inequality threatens the nation's identity, its core narrative. Scholars of international relations call this *ontological security*.

Threats that cause a country's identity crisis are felt as deeply as threats to its economic or national security. The reactions are the same, too. The state uses its instruments of power to reduce the risk, convey strength, and reestablish a sense of normalcy. Law enforcement is typically employed at the tip of the spear for domestic threats, putting them into confrontational relationships with the very communities it's supposed to protect and serve.

Questions about race and law enforcement in the United States today are neither about whether white and Black people hate each other nor about whether there's a cultural bias in law enforcement against Black people in particular. It is decidedly a question about the duties of the state to its citizens, especially those who have been historically excluded, and about the state's acceptance of accountability when it falls short.

Racism remains a national Achilles' heel because it forces a confrontation with our identity and demands that the proper balance of liberty and security be available to all citizens regardless of their race or ethnicity. The protests spawned by George Floyd's murder put a spotlight on this quandary that Black Americans have always had an eye on. Would the people reject abuse of power by state-sanctioned agents, even when it happens to those we've been told deserve it? The protests showed small signs of multiracial solidarity among the general population—something that the nation rarely sees; it's a good sign. It gave us reason to believe that the moment might've served as an inflection point, and perhaps a tipping point, too.

. . .

THE UNITED STATES IS A DIFFERENT place today from what it was when the new decade dawned. A president was twice impeached. A global pandemic killed over a million of us. The economy has seesawed while unemployment and inflation keep us all on edge and economically insecure. The role of racism in the present-day United States—and what, if anything, is owed for historical wrongs—continues to capture public attention. There is no going back to pre-2020 America. New is here, and the choices we make now will shape the American way of life for those who come next.

Taking the need for structural reforms seriously and ensuring protections from state powers will lead to better outcomes, a better country. The public sees the matter of overpolicing and of racism in the criminal justice system much more clearly now than it once did. The nation has changed. A poll taken after Floyd's murder showed that most Americans—most white, most Hispanic, and most Black Americans—were more concerned about the actions of the police that led to nationwide protests than they were that some protests turned violent. By a margin of two to one,

Americans believed that the criminal justice system treated white Americans better than it did Black Americans and that the police killings of Black citizens in recent years were signs of a broader problem. Most Americans—a majority of each racial group—thought that race was a major factor in Floyd's death, thought that police were too often not held accountable for misconduct, and supported measures to mitigate the use of deadly force.[5]

And, as if on cue, the politician and sensationalized media entered the scene. They looked to translate the public energy into partisan policy and must-see TV. Some progressives demanded that police forces across the country be defunded or abolished. Their proposals benefited from videos of peaceful protesters being met with swinging batons, tear gas and smoke, rubber bullets, polycarbonate shields that pushed citizens to the ground, the front end of police SUVs, and even the front hooves of mounted patrols. Some on the right preferred that more militarized police forces, and even the military itself, face down the demonstrators. That view was aided by raucous rioters destroying private property, opportunists raiding businesses, and angry folks setting police cars ablaze.

The policy fights will rage as usual, but we shouldn't allow them to distract us from what happened in the country. At a time when political and partisan polarizations seem to doom the prospect of good governance, Americans across lines that typically divide us came together daily, for weeks on end, to demand a change in behavior by the state and its agents, aligning us more closely to our professed principles. The collective outrage at the racial injustice and abuse of power that fueled the summer of 2020 is a testimony of American progress.

Work remains. Will the government heed the people's will? How can police departments across the country keep the faith of the American people? Political institutions and actors need to adjust; political and electoral incentive structures need to be people-first. Citizens need to consider all the ways in which racial injustice harms the American experiment.

NOT LONG AFTER FLOYD'S MURDER, there was a photo circulating of, on one side, former 49ers quarterback Colin Kaepernick kneeling during the national anthem and, on the other side, Minnesota police officer Derek Chauvin casually kneeling on the neck of George Floyd. The striking image implicitly asks about the value of Black life. And about the authority of Black people to demand different.

It reminded me of the conversation back in the Pentagon during my last week in uniform. I told my colleague that since my sixteenth birthday, I'd been pulled over about forty times by police—almost always escaping citations by intentionally handing over my military ID along with my driver's license. I told him of the experiences of family members and friends who'd also had the uncanny misfortune of attracting undue police attention. I told him of the night a Black & Mild and a recently expired license landed me in jail.

He asked if I thought most of the confrontations between unarmed Black people and police were just a matter of bad apples. I told him, "No."

He asked if I thought that all police were racist. No.

But to his question of whether police treated Black people differently—of whether I believed that racial injustice exists—the answer could only be yes.

CHAPTER 6

Semiquin

Every July fourth, two things are sure to happen. The first is that a buddy is going to post his annual rant to social media.

"It is not 'the Fourth of July.' It is Independence Day," he'll write. "That's what we are celebrating. Independence."

He's making the point that we should call the observance by its name rather than by the date it occurs on. It's followed by a pithy and sometimes irreverent flourish about why *the Fourth* doesn't make sense. One year it was "It's not Cinco de Mayo. This isn't Mexico." Another year he similarly noted that we don't call Christmas *the twenty-fifth of December* or Veterans Day *the eleventh of November*. "So why are we doing it for Independence Day?" Also fair. And once he used some dry humor to note that July second—the day that colonies declared their freedom from Great Britain[1]—is the proper anniversary for the nation's independence, as if to say, "'The Fourth' is the wrong name for a celebration happening on the wrong date."

The second is that Frederick Douglass will be invoked. All week long, my Black peoples will be sharing his famous speech, "What to the Slave is the Fourth of July?" from 1852, when slavery was very much alive and well. About halfway through the address, he asked an exasperated rhetorical question of the white abolitionists: "What have I, or those I represent, to do with your national independence?"[2] He called the United States hypocritical for championing liberty while pardoning the ownership of people and giving safe passage to the slave driver's caravan. Douglass suggested Independence Day reminded the enslaved Black person of "the gross injustice and cruelty to which he is the constant victim. To him, your celebration is a sham; your boasted liberty, an unholy license; your national greatness, swelling vanity. . . ."

Many Black folks feel Douglass's words from more than 170 years ago deep in their bones today, reminded on the holiday that liberty is different for them. And yet, though it gets less attention than it should, Black critique of the United States is shot through with hope and optimism. Douglass, as usual, modeled it. His speech also extolled the virtues of the Declaration and stated his faith in the United States plainly: "I do not despair of this country."

We do not either. We cannot. It is the only one we have.

When my white buddy's Independence Day reminder is read alongside excerpts from Douglass's speech, there's a story in the distinction. Though we engage in the collective ritual—convening at pools and beaches and cookouts and nightcaps and fireworks—some are celebrating America and being American while others are staking an ownership claim and asserting their place in an America once denied to people like them. This matters because why we mark anniversaries is more meaningful than how, though the *how* gets all the attention. The country's rituals and symbols become the focus of manufactured and politicized outrage about everything from flag lapel pins to national anthem etiquette, distracting us from the root problem. What does the day mean and who does it belong to?

When the different answers to *what the Fourth means to me* are considered, they gather into one of two camps. One leads with reckoning. The other with pride. We disagree on whether the nation is primarily something we should be proud of or the thing that must be contended with to achieve liberty. Understanding that difference helps us understand the United States' central challenge: getting a diverse people to share both a national identity and aspirations for the future without muting their respective group history or culture.

This is why anniversaries matter. How we mark them and which ones we choose to commemorate tell us something about who we are, who we think we are, and who we hope to be. Celebration of a nation's birthday is an important civic and social ritual. Societies need these to reaffirm a sense of identity and connection among its people. When people opt out of these rituals and celebrations, it is received as an explicit rejection of both the experience and the people participating in it. This is why *how* we mark the date is important—it is public, observable, and, therefore, social and political. And it is ripe for superficial conflicts masking that we've still not agreed on who are the *us*. Whether someone stands or kneels during the national anthem becomes more important than why. National rituals and symbols are hijacked and used to divide us.

If anniversaries are rich with insights about a people and a country, then milestone commemorations over time should tell us something about the nature of a nation. With four fifty-year anniversaries under our belt and the next one coming in just a couple years—the semiquincentennial, or 250th year of independence—there's enough material to find a nation's character. Grander sweeps of time provide perspective. Is there a bend toward justice or toward something else less laudable and poetic? Has the nation's nature changed, or has it simply adjusted its membership requirements? We know the right answers to give, the ones that affirm our values are true and that we're fulfilling our national destiny. But a more accurate diagnosis is found in the patterns that emerge over milestone national anniversaries.

So allons-y.

. . .

OF THE FOUR FIFTY-YEAR ANNIVERSARIES TO DATE—1826, the semicentennial; 1876, the centennial; 1926, the sesqui-centennial; and 1976, the bicentennial—only the last occurred after the end of slavery and Jim Crow. What must it be like to watch a nation celebrate freedom and independence while you are bound at the wrists and ankles or pushed to back seats and broken water fountains? What story does a nation tell itself that makes this hypocrisy acceptable?

Who does America think it is?

When reading all the ways different people have marked the nation's benchmark anniversaries, I find that three themes burst through: *pride, reckoning,* and *aspiration.* Pride comes across as a nation that's proud of overcoming all of history's hardships. It is proud of where it has been even when it isn't proud of what it has done. For all the nation's missteps, pride believes the United States is ultimately a cause to be celebrated.

When reckoning appears, the original sin is never far behind. It is the nation's defining paradox, asking how a nation founded on the idea of equality continued enslaving people. Even on other issues, like discrimination on the basis of sex, gender, and sexual orientation or class conflicts between the rich and working class, failures on racial equality are the reference point that advocates for gender equality and a fair economy appeal to. How can the country make its past wrongs right? Or, others might say, we should acknowledge that it has already done so—and now too much is being asked.

Aspiration dreams of a nation where its people feel like they belong, where there is a shared vision for what the nation will be. It is a promise to posterity: we will leave this place better than we found it. And it is an ode to the past, telling its stories in the hopes that we don't have to learn things the hard way, again. It aspires to exceptionalism, but a tolerant and humble version that makes room for others and leads by example.

Pride. Reckoning. Aspiration. The country is always grappling with what it's supposed to take pride in. With what it's done that requires reckoning. With what it aspires to be and for whom. The answers to these questions are found in the moods and rhetoric at anniversaries. They are where the soul of a nation shows itself.

THE SEMICENTENNIAL, US@50

For those who believed the creation of the United States was a divine occurrence, they took the events of July 4, 1826, as proof. On that date—the day the country turned fifty—two of its most iconic figures from the founding generation died: Thomas Jefferson and John Adams. The president on that day, John Quincy Adams, invoked the Lord's hand in an executive order marking the deaths of his father and Jefferson: "A coincidence of circumstances so wonderful gives confidence to the belief that the patriotic efforts of these illustrious men were Heaven directed, and furnishes a new seal to the hope that the prosperity of these States is under the special protection of a kind Providence."[3] It was an affirmation that the United States was ordained, favored. The deaths of two of its earliest presidents on this day weren't a coincidence; they were deemed a sign of the Lord passing by, sweeping up battle-weary disciples. These are the things myths are made of.

Anniversaries are commemorations that begin with an implicit announcement: *Let us gather for the recitation of our truth.* In 1826, Speaker of the House John W. Taylor did the customary thing and recounted the nation's mythic march to independence. Americans' desire for equality was so strong, the story went, that it compelled separation from Great Britain, fueled by the righteousness of the cause and the fervor of the people. Taylor explained that our military successes, population growth, and economic prosperity were proof of the goodness of the creation. He granted that there were imperfections, like the unprincipled men who practiced nasty politics. "These partial evils, perhaps necessarily incident to our free institutions, are but the spots on our sun's disc," he said before moving on. It was a "momentous truth," Taylor declared, that the United States existed to be "an example to mankind."⁴ We may have been imperfect, but we were chosen.

The problem of slavery was ignored altogether.

In his anniversary address, Representative Edward Everett from Massachusetts also deified previous generations as a way of identifying pride in our founding narratives. "The age of commemoration is at hand," he told a crowd gathered in Cambridge. "The voice of our fathers' blood begins to cry to us, from beneath the soil which it moistened. Time is bringing forward, in their proper relief, the men and the deeds of that high-souled day."⁵ He went on to recount all the blood spilled in the war for independence, suggesting—as Lincoln would decades later—that the blood sacrifice cleansed the nation's aims. It was lore.

He, too, made no mention of slavery. And we know why. Earlier that year in Congress, he gave a three-hour speech that characterized slavery as neither immoral nor against the tenets of religion. He couched it as a necessary but unfortunate evil. The speech was politically costly and haunted him for the rest of his political career.

Others made different choices, choosing to lead with reckoning instead of pride. More than two decades before Frederick Douglass asked what the Fourth meant to the slave, a white Presbyterian minister in New York declared the approaching semicentennial "the year of jubilee, but not for Africans."⁶ He accused the United States of holding the

Declaration in one hand and chains and whips in the other. In Vermont, a professor who would go on to run the state's newspaper of record called slavery an evil that the nation had gotten used to, one that "affixe[d] guilt to the nation, and unless removed, [would] bring upon us the vengeance of a benevolent God."[7] Another minister in Rochester chastised, "This fiftieth year of American Independence has not found the principle of equal rights universally confirmed within a territory called free. Still the dark stain of African bondage is not wiped away."[8]

Josiah Quincy, the mayor of Boston and soon the president of Harvard College, delivered a semicentennial address that painted a picture of aspiration as relevant then as now. The speech was both grand in its praise of the American Revolution and stark in its warnings against putting political parties ahead of the nation. It was the nation's duty at fifty to honor the founders by maintaining the genius of what they created. And though it was natural for people to separate into factions, Quincy echoed concerns that this could be the country's undoing. He accused those who chose party over principles and who reflexively hated people in the other party of being "false to the genius and character of our revolution."[9] Doomed were the nations "who form parties on men, and not upon principles."

Government officials were all pride and aspiration. Ministers and abolitionists, reckoning and aspiration. The convergence of the three was hard to find.

THE CENTENNIAL, US@100

The deaths of two of the nation's founders welcomed the end of the first fifty years. The massacre of Black men in Aiken County, South Carolina, greeted the anniversary of the next fifty years.

On July 4, 1876, in the predominantly Black town of Hamburg, the local freedmen militia had gathered for the Fourth of July, Independence Day. After the Civil War, many Black people used the day to celebrate freedom from slavery. While the unit was marching in the holiday parade, a couple white farmers attempted to break through the formation. It was neither a mistake nor patriotic exuberance. It was an intentional provocation. They were Red Shirts, a white supremacist paramilitary organization. And it worked. When all was said and done, Black militiamen were rounded up and randomly selected for lynching.

The nation's centennial was a commercial affair. The major exposition in Philadelphia was the first world's fair held in the United States. Inventions debuted here that would remake the future—the telephone, the first QWERTY-keyboard typewriter, a mechanical calculator. Popcorn. Ice-cream soda. Everything was new. And for sale.

A market quickly opened for the centennial's story. Was it an appreciative history of revolution and our founding? A celebration of distinctively American freedom and liberty and prosperity, with cookouts and fireworks and storytelling? Or a promise to those who'd been excluded that America and its opportunity were available to them, too?[10]

Pride bloomed in its usual fashion. President Ulysses S. Grant issued a proclamation for the centennial that dripped with divine purpose. It was to be a day of "public religious and devout thanksgiving to Almighty God for the blessings which ha[d] been bestowed upon us as a nation during the century of our existence."[11] It seemed, instead, to be one of celebrating and partying. An editorial in Chicago lamented that "not one out of one hundred kn[ew] anything about the origin of national independence." Another said nothing remained of the day but hangovers and boys with firecrackers.[12]

Robert Winthrop—once a senator from Massachusetts and Speaker of the House—told a crowd in Boston that though the United States could not forget the stain of slavery, it should be proud to have conquered it. There had never been "a more tremendous, a more dreadful, problem submitted to a nation for solution," he said, "than that which this institution involved for the United States of America."[13] The country had done a hard thing. We should be proud of that.

That pride was to be expressed in prosperity. And civic identity started to look like that of a consumer, of a customer. The seeds of the idea that became the American Dream were planted at the centennial. Industry. Ingenuity. Prosperity. Progress. If we could not find a shared pride in the past, then maybe there was some to be shared in envisioning the possibilities of tomorrow, the great economic possibilities of it all. For us all.

New technology was welcome; new political ideas were not. Suffragists interrupted the reading of the Declaration in Philadelphia with their own, stating, "While the nation is buoyant with patriotism, and all hearts are attuned to praise," it must be remembered that "all women still suffer the degradation of disfranchisement."[14] Change quaked the country. Commercialization. The war. Black people in Congress. Reunification. Women. Reconstruction. A lot was happening.

And these historical remembrances troubled the focus on the future. Southerners arrived at the Centennial Exposition to see murals of the United States' victory over the Confederacy. Bygones were supposed to bygones, not the source of a new national myth. A newspaper editorial in Virginia lamented: "There ought not to be anything there which revives the unpleasant memories of the late bloody struggle inside the nation."[15] It was a feeling held in much of the South.

One historian notes that being a good American "had evolved to the point that most Midwesterners recognized the patriotism in spectacle, the liberty in recreation, and the freedom in leisure."[16] Another comments, "A recurring theme in southern anti-Centennial rhetoric was that the Exhibition was nothing more than a northern money-making scam."[17] Leisure was a point of pride, proof of our exceptionalism. To others, it was evidence of decaying virtue.

Reckoning at the centennial had an aspirational Black voice. Though the people themselves were noticeably absent at the Centennial Exposition, either as guests or as features in the national story, their stories were used to show the nation's obligation. Black struggle and resilience insisted on inclusion in the national myth. In an Independence Day address, Black clergyman and historian George Washington Williams declared freedmen owed no debt to the country because emancipation was neither gift nor loan—citizenship was purchased by Black work and sacrifice. He believed it was the demand for equality in the "soul of the negro soldier that made this country forever free."[18] But, he cautioned, "The evil influences of the institution linger among us. Its impress was made upon the souls as well as upon the bodies of its subjects. It will take years before this country will outgrow the scars of slavery."[19]

At a July 4 event in Chester, Pennsylvania, prominent Black researcher and doctor Isaac Coates noted that no nation was perfect, but he was proud slavery's reckoning was a domestic one, saying, "I rejoice as an American that it was fought on the soil of America—decidedly for freedom—for all mankind—for all ages!" If we are genuine in our beliefs, and our actions follow suit, he said, "then, indeed, shall our great country be elevated to the most exalted and sublime eminence among the nation of the earth."[20]

Meanwhile, the Red Shirts in Hamburg, South Carolina, interrupted Black people's July 4 celebration. The initial confrontation was resolved easily enough, but the Red Shirts sued the freedmen for blocking the passage of white men. And they showed up armed and en masse to the court proceedings to demand that the freedmen's guns be taken. Before long, thirty Black freedmen were holed up in the National Guard armory and surrounded by a hundred Red Shirts with a cannon. The Red Shirts took the armory, put the freedmen in a circle, and made a game of randomly killing several, one by one. Six Black people and one Red Shirt were killed in the Hamburg Massacre. More white supremacist violence occurred in the lead-up to the 1876 president election, which invited the end of Reconstruction. President Grant called the scene at Hamburg "cruel, bloodthirsty, wanton, unprovoked, and uncalled for."[21] He wrote that every state had the same right as any other, "unless it may be the right to kill negroes and republicans without fear of punishment."[22] A nation still guilty as sin.

After the election and Compromise of 1877, federal troops' protection of Black people in the South dropped off. If Jefferson's and Adams's deaths signaled the death of the Founding Era's version of exclusive democracy, then the centennial was a statement on how exclusive it would remain. The lack of consensus led to a siege of factionalism, racism, sectarianism, and rampant political violence across the former Confederate states. These were not reasons for commemoration. Instead, as one nineteenth-century historian described the centennial, citizens lost interest in the nation's origins and complex history, instead preferring "the pomp and showiness of postbellum commemorations and the whitewashed history reprinted in local newspapers."[23]

The town of Hamburg, South Carolina, no longer exists. Between the racism and violence and routine flooding due to a lack of levees, few people stayed. In 1916, a still-standing monument was erected to commemorate the hero of the clash. It was for the one Red Shirt who died, giving his life for "the highest ideal of Anglo-Saxon civilization," thereby assuring "the children of his beloved land the supremacy of that ideal." The Black militiamen who were killed while working as federal agents are not mentioned at all. On the site where the massacre took place, today there is a golf course. It sits behind a drive of the American Dream, a row of million-dollar homes on the northside bank of the Savannah River.

THE SESQUICENTENNIAL, US@150

The headline of the August 25, 1926, edition of *Variety* magazine labeled the sesquicentennial AMERICA'S GREATEST FLOP.[24] Philadelphia hosted a world's fair again. This time, though, interest was relatively low. The exposition fell into a twenty-million-dollar debt that forced the auctioning of its assets.

The Roaring Twenties in the United States was a time of rapid technological advancement, doubling the nation's wealth and its urbanization, and massive cultural revolutions in the arts and across society. It also saw the resurgence of the Ku Klux Klan, a constitutional ban on alcohol to counter fears of moral erosion, and negative reactions to people immigrating to the United States and migrating out of the South. Whereas the centennial was just a few years after the Civil War, the 1920s took place during a burgeoning cultural war along class, gender, racial, regional, political, and sectarian lines. The nature of the nation was being tested. By the decade's end, the Great Depression had knocked the glitter off American prosperity.

President Calvin Coolidge delivered a sesquicentennial address where he reminded the country of its blessed genesis. He offered a long passage recounting the dawn and arrival of independence. He connected the massive shifts happening in the country to its founding, saying, "We live in an age of science and of abounding accumulation of material things. These did not create our Declaration. Our Declaration created them."[25] As was standard practice at these anniversaries, the deification of the founders came next. "If we are to maintain the great heritage which has been bequeathed to us," Coolidge preached, "we must be like-minded as the fathers who created it. We must not sink into a pagan materialism. We must cultivate the reverence which they had for the things that are holy."[26]

He put the centennial of Jefferson's death on par with the nation's 150th birthday, using the occasion to praise the

Declaration's author by bringing up his opposition to slavery. Coolidge, whose birthday was Independence Day, said Jefferson paved the way both for democracy and for slavery's "ultimate extinction on American soil."[27] This was slavery's first appearance in a presidential benchmark anniversary address, and it was a success story. It became the hard problem that the country solved, making its way into the national myths as further evidence of our exceptionalism. It provided yet another reason the country should be celebrated, another reason for pride.

Despite the president's remarks, mentions of slavery, Jim Crow, and the Civil War during the anniversary remained rare. The partisan politics of the day adjusted to the Great Migration's arrivals, who altered local, state, and national electoral politics. The political parties' civil rights platforms became regional hodgepodges, making the parties largely indistinguishable on the issue. Coolidge may not be bold enough for us today, but he was not milquetoast on race. He was ahead of the times, noting in a 1924 speech at Howard University that "the colored people have repeatedly proved their devotion to the high ideals of our country" and "the black man showed himself the same kind of citizen, moved by the same kind of patriotism, as the white man."[28] But such strong pronouncements were missing from the sesquicentennial. The anniversary was for recounting and adding to the nation's lore, not stirring the pot on race issues that already had the country on edge.

Reckoning, as a result, remained a difficult ask. The threats of consumerism and partisanship that roiled the Roaring Twenties were more about managing a bustling nation than shortcomings to be reckoned with. Though capitalism and democracy in the United States have always been bedfellows, treating the two as if they're inextricably entangled commoditizes democracy before it democratizes the economy. It erases the difference between freedom and prosperity, and we become a nation of *citizen consumers*—a term coined by historian Lizabeth Cohen. She frames it as a phenomenon in which "Americans are asking of the public domain, 'Am I getting my money's worth?' rather than 'What's best for America?'"[29] When the sesquicentennial anniversary arrived, the Nineteenth Amendment granting women the right to vote had been ratified a few years earlier, new discriminatory immigration and citizenship laws had passed, and the economy was thriving. Americans were having a good time. They were dancing, styling themselves anew, and shaking off socially conservative expectations. Slavery had been solved. It was understandable if reckoning took a back seat.

But then there was Harlem.

The Great Migration brought Black people out of the South and to points in the Northeast and Midwest. High concentrations of them were stuffed into small geographic spaces, and despite the discriminatory policies that created and maintained their neighborhoods, they became hotbeds of creativity. The Harlem Renaissance was born. This cultural movement gave new expression to the Black experience, and the demand for reckoning permeated the music, the writing, the performing. In 1926, Langston Hughes published *The Weary Blues*, which contained a poem earmarked for the sesquicentennial. In "I, Too," Hughes used a dinner analogy to speak to Black people's second-class citizenship, saying that the darker people once made to eat in the kitchen would soon have a place at the table. And when that happened, there would be no going back. "Besides," Hughes said with a swag characteristic of the era, "They'll see how beautiful I am, / And be ashamed— / I, too, am America."[30]

Black people became part of the national myth as the object of other people's heroism. But Black people found agency in their own publications and shared their views of pride, reckoning, and aspiration. In the sesquicentennial issue of the Baltimore newspaper *Afro-American*, a banner across the top read 150TH ANNIVERSARY OF THE SIGNING OF THE DECLARATION OF INDEPENDENCE—"WE WHO STROVE FOR FREE AND INDEPENDENT STATES MUST OURSELVES BE FREE AND UNOPPRESSED." [31] The *Monitor* in Omaha, Nebraska, reported on exhibits at the exposition in Philadelphia lauding "Negro Achievement" in spite of the racism they had long faced.[32] And the *Richmond Planet* remarked on the beauty of hearing "Lift Every Voice and Sing" at sesquicentennial celebrations.[33]

At the sesquicentennial, the race question became more

complicated. No longer was it confined to the issue of slavery. Now there were policy issues to consider beyond abolition. It was about work and pay, housing and school, laws and courts, voting and belonging and fairness. What was once a question of emancipation was now one of liberation. In this way, the sesquicentennial did indeed represent America's Greatest Flop, proof of its missed opportunity to get emancipation right while pride, reckoning, and aspiration took on a decidedly economic character.

THE BICENTENNIAL, US@200

If Americans could have said anything at the bicentennial that they could have said at the founding, it was this: '76 *is a mess*. In 1776, battles with British forces dotted the colonial map. The Brits played on racial, ethnic, and class tensions to try and break the revolution. In 1876, a contested presidential election used a backroom deal to decide the winner, who weakened federal troop protection for Black Southerners. Democracy, in both system and idea, proved as corruptible as the people who led it. In 1976, the nation was still reeling from the historic resignation of President Richard Nixon, and Gerald Ford was president, though he had never won a presidential election as the party nominee or as a running mate. Americans were upset about Vietnam. A cultural revolution followed the civil rights and gender equality movements, and the 1970s was fertile ground for blossoming countercultures.

Though Americans hadn't chosen him for president, Ford, a former college football player and naval officer, stepped into the role for bicentennial celebrations like a pro. Two of his speeches to two very different audiences spoke to the balancing act he attempted to manage between the nation's origin story and its changing demography. At the National Archives, he praised the founders, the genius of a democratic republic, and the sacrifice it took to make it reality. "The great promise of the Declaration," Ford said to the country, "requires far more than the patriot sacrifices of the American Revolution, more than the legal stabilizer of the Constitution, more than Lincoln's successful answer to the question of whether a nation so conceived and so dedicated could long endure."[34]

Two days later, Ford gave an address at a naturalization ceremony held at Jefferson's Monticello and distinguished himself from his predecessors' anniversary addresses. He added "nation of immigrants" to the bicentennial's narrative. He told these new citizens that immigrants were an invaluable source of national strength. And that "such transfusions of traditions and cultures, as well as of blood, have made America unique among nations and Americans a new kind of people."[35] He nodded to a young America's "stubborn blind spots" that kept Black people and women out of the democracy for too long. But he moved on quickly. "This is not the day, however, to deplore our shortcomings or to regret that not all new citizens have been welcomed as you are here today," he said, seeing the moment as appropriate for pride, not for reckoning. "The essential fact is that the United States—as a national policy and in the hearts of most Americans—has been willing to absorb anyone from anywhere."[36] This narrative had worked itself into the national story, sugarcoating and all.

Ford's rhetoric on pride stuck to the script. Others took up reckoning. In his bicentennial address, Theodore Hesburgh, a Catholic priest and president of Notre Dame University, said it clearly, "I have tarried, overly you might think, on the black experience, because I believe that it is here that America really will make the worldwide breakthrough for justice and freedom."[37] In a speech for the ages, congressional representative Barbara Jordan from Texas asked, "In 1976, are we to be one people bound together by common spirit, sharing in a common endeavor, or will we become a divided nation?"[38] In the *New York Times*' bicentennial day paper, Toni Morrison published "The Black Experience; A Slow Walk of Trees (as Grandmother Would Say) Hopeless (as Grandfather Would Say)," the most beautiful essay of the day. It was a family story working as an allegory for the Black experience. Progress came slowly, like a canopy of trees that creeped across landscapes little by little, year after year. But, for others, incremental progress was not a sign of promise. The slow walk, instead, was reason enough for a people's faith to lag, justification for losing hope.

Aspiration at the bicentennial assumed its usual form. Groups held competing celebrations across the ideological spectrum, competing to remake—or profit from—a new American narrative. The anniversary was fully politicized, despite Ford's attempts at avoiding polarization. Black folks, now in the halls of Congress to make official pronouncements, put additional teeth on the call for an aspiration that reckons with the past. Representative Charles Rangel of New York offered, "If the Bicentennial is some kind of self-congratulatory celebration, it is frivolous and meaningless to the Black community. . . . If they're going to have a party, we're going to be there to blow the birthday candles out."[39] It is only meaningful, Rangel argued, "if the Bicentennial can be seen as a rededication to full equality."

It could certainly be seen as commercialized. It featured the sort of holiday sales and advertising that are commonplace today. Some went further, rebranding the bicentennial to "buy-centennial." Want to show national pride? Want to feel good about the future? Want to remain optimistic despite the chaotic world around you? Spend some money. Buy some stuff.

Reverend Hesburgh grounded the anniversary by restating the Promise of America, and he highlighted racial inequality as the chief obstacle to a shared aspiration: "If we can achieve freedom and justice for all here, then maybe there is hope for the rest of the world. This is our greatest Bicentennial message to mankind everywhere."[40]

• • •

THE OLD BLACK COUPLE AT the heart of Morrison's essay gives voice to the open question that has accompanied every benchmark anniversary. The title is the grandmother's phrase to describe the look and feel of things when taken into perspective. It is born of the wisdom that the true nature of a thing is harder to hide over grand sweeps of time. To survive, to persevere, is to be human. It's as true for people as for nations.

The grandfather sees things differently. He asks why we should not be hopeless. If race still remains at the core of the nation's problems two centuries after independence, why should we believe tomorrow will be different? Any progress that doesn't involve the end of violence, penalties for discrimination, and accessible and fair systems of justice and democracy isn't really progress at all. A commemorative coin doesn't change people's material experiences.

They are both right. It's going to be Independence Day one way or another. As 2026 approaches, and the nation prepares for its semiquincentennial and 250th year, the slow walk will continue. And some on the journey will wonder if the day ever comes when they, too, can celebrate achieving independence—liberation—on the Fourth of July.

CHAPTER 7

Out of Many, Twoness

I met Bigger Thomas in high school. We were in history class together, the only two Black people in the room. My classmates didn't understand him and seemed hesitant to engage. When he spoke, their eyes often turned to me. I was more familiar to them, having grown up in their neighborhoods and been one of a very few Black mainstays in their classes. They were looking, I think, to see how to properly react, or maybe to see if he spoke for me, too. Sometimes I tried interpreting, but there was only so much that could be said or done to help them see the world from Bigger's vantage. And I was a teenager. I hadn't lived enough to really know. But the last thing that I was going to do in that room full of white people was suggest that I didn't know how it felt to be Black in America. And in that class, on that question, Bigger was an authority.

Of course, Bigger Thomas is the main character in the

historic 1940 novel *Native Son*. It was assigned by our brilliant teacher Dr. Goodwin, the sort of man who was so passionate about history that you'd find him between classes always in the middle of a sentence—talking to a math teacher, a cafeteria worker, the football coach, anyone—about some historical event. His passion for history filled the room, providing soft landings when the harder truths about the country knocked us down. Still, he was a man of his era and station. He knew the history that made Bigger possible, but he did not know Bigger.

When we finished the book, Goodwin assigned an expository essay. I got an A. The guy who sat next to me in class was Mormon and, on seeing my grade, said with a friendly chuckle, "Of course you got an A! You really think he was gonna mark you down for anything in an essay about Black people? That's like me writing a paper about Mormons. Guaranteed A." Being something makes you a kind of scholar in it. But too often shared experience confers an authority, usually unwarranted and unearned, to speak for all others.

I do not know what it's like to live in a rat-infested one-bedroom apartment with three other people. Bigger does. I do not know what it's like to be so angry with the world that you beat up your friend, making him lick a knife's edge in the process. Or what it's like to have so much fear of white people that you accidentally smother a white woman with a pillow after stealing a kiss, dismantle the body, fabricate a tale of the murder by a Communist, and then kill your Black girlfriend after telling her the whole story. Bigger does; I do not.

I know what it's like to be in a room of people of a different race and class and feel out of place, lesser than. I know the haunting feeling that cautions against the smallest missteps that might attract negative attention. I know the stereotypes about Black masculinity—that it's inherently violent and hypersexual and mischievous and shiftless—and how those descriptions enter rooms teeming with second glances and unseen nudges long before I arrive. These are the realities that Bigger faces and that send him into destructive panics. I do not understand why he responds in his way, but the world that makes him feels familiar to me, too. Nothing about the Black experience today is universal, but a lot of it is shared. In his 1955 book *Notes of a Native Son*, James Baldwin wrote, "No American Negro exists who does not have his private Bigger Thomas living in the skull . . . [He is] compelled to accept the fact that this dark and dangerous and unloved stranger is part of himself forever."[1] Bigger comes from a people that have long been considered a problem. He is the problem come to life, brought to life.

That was hard for me to accept and understand. Goodwin mentioned there was another book—W. E. B. Du Bois's *The Souls of Black Folk*—that would help us further interrogate the world that raised Bigger. I went straight to the bookstore after school and devoured *Souls* in a weekend. On

Monday morning I showed up to class with *Souls* in tow. Goodwin beamed like a proud parent.

After some light conversation as other students filed in, he asked, "What part of it has stayed with you most?"

"The question," I answered without a second of hesitation.

His brow furrowed. "The question?" He was a rapt audience.

"Yeah, the question. 'How does it feel to be a problem?'"

He gave an exaggerated nod, the sort that signals, *Ah yes, of course.* It was not the response I'd hoped for. I wanted something stronger. Like this:

"Well?"

SOULS WAS A GUT PUNCH. Taking in all the new ideas and new ways of seeing things was jarring. At times, Du Bois takes the scenic route to an insight that would've been better served with a beeline. But the writing is beautiful; it's all part of his charm.

The first paragraph holds the question that guides the whole book. You can see the chuckle in his pen as he remembers all the ways white people have gently assured him that his race doesn't bother them. "To the real question, 'How does it feel to be a problem,'" he says, "I answer seldom a word."[2] The reader gets the same treatment. Du Bois only gives vague descriptions. *Strange experience. Peculiar sensation.*

The passage originally appeared in an essay he authored in 1897. Du Bois was just twenty-nine at the time and wrapping up landmark research in Philadelphia en route to a professorship at Atlanta University. Today we know it as Clark—well, *we* know it as Clark. And that minor distinction gets to his central point: *Black American* holds two core identities, and that sometimes necessitates clarifying who the *we* are. And reconciling those two identities is the existential test facing Black people in the United States. And it is the answer to America's potential as both a nation and an idea. Here's how he describes it in *Souls'* most famous passage:

> It is a peculiar sensation, this double-consciousness, this sense of always looking at one's self through the eyes of others, of measuring one's soul by the tape of a world that looks on in amused contempt and pity. One ever feels his two-ness—an American, a Negro; two souls, two thoughts, two unreconciled strivings; two warring ideals in one dark body, whose dogged strength alone keeps it from being torn asunder.[3]

It's trademark Du Bois. Provocative in the simplest, most poetic way. The United States had so actively oppressed Black people that its identity became connected to it. So a people's desire for liberty naturally worked in opposition to the American interest. How, then, could someone be both? How is it possible to be Black and American?

And yet, as one, there's nothing about my being Black that's incompatible with my being American. The two were born together, raised together. I don't know how to be one without a touch of the other. For folks who feel the same, what do *twoness* and *double-consciousness* and *a nation at war with its nation* mean, then?

· · ·

MY SISTER AND I WERE born in the 1970s and entered elementary school in the eighties. Everything was scary. Weather. The Russians. Strangers.

It was the decade when Halloween costumes were made of shower-curtain material, smelling of vinyl. We trick-or-treated for a few years before our church decided that Halloween was the devil. There were horror movie characters with names like Jason, Freddie, Chuckie, and Michael Myers. None of them really scared my sister and me. There were only two things that terrified these two little children of churchgoing parents in the South: the devil and the Klan.

It was also the decade when Halloween candy and white vans became major areas of concern in the United States. Long before social media, the grapevine and the evening news carried stories of sewing needles and drugs and razor blades and poison being suspected in trick-or-treaters' candy.[4] Mild panic ensued. In some places, X-ray stations were set up to scan candy for foreign objects. Strangers were not to be trusted. There were after-school specials and public service announcements with McGruff the Crime Dog warning children about the hazards of getting into cars with strangers. Plain white vans. Weird guys in shades offering candy. Stranger danger!

The one vehicle scarier than a white van, for us, was an old pickup. A clown in a white van looked more fun than what we knew was in those old pickup trucks. Racist good ol' boys drove them; they were mean and everywhere. Decades later, when the news broke that three white supremacists kidnapped James Byrd Jr.—beat him before peeing and defecating on him, chained and dragged him for three miles behind their vehicle, and then threw his headless torso in front of a Black church—I already knew what they were driving. That kind of knowledge has a history, a set of real experiences. When Black people are asked about their first racist incident or first time being called a nigger, too many answers involve white guys in pickup trucks.

My sister and I shared many of the experiences and fears of the children of our day, no matter their race or ethnicity. The white van meant the same thing to most of us. White men in pickups, however, meant something different, something very specific to our skin and our safety. That is a very particular way of understanding the world. It's a wisdom born out of double-consciousness—of measuring yourself in the eyes of the other world, understanding how you are perceived, and using that information to keep safe and, hopefully, thrive.

This isn't a problem as much as it's an intelligence. And

it's why twoness, as typically conceived, has always felt too one-dimensional for me. The way the world sees us is important to understand, but it should not be our tape measure. Our challenge is taking all the unique things we know about being Black and American and using them to the benefit of both. The problem is when people don't believe it's possible.

That's how I would answer the question of how it feels to be a problem, if Goodwin were here to ask. And it's how I would've explained to my classmates why the craze got Bigger Thomas.

HOW DOES IT FEEL, THROUGH no fault of your own, to bear the mark of a country's original sin? This is another way of asking the idea Du Bois was after. As a veteran, wearing the country's uniform, I understand the question differently.

Few things confound twoness and the nation's myths like a Black person in a military uniform. Military service confers social capital and a particular prestige not available through other types of civic engagement. It provides a claim to the title of American like few other things. The mesh of race and uniform—the paradox, hypocrisy—was often too much for the country. During World War I, many Black American soldiers serving overseas weren't allowed to fight under the United States flag. The segregated 93rd Infantry Battalion was forced to serve under the flag of France, wear blue French helmets, and use French equipment.[5] And when army leadership received word that the French were treating the Black soldiers with more respect, they demanded that Jim Crow practices be imposed.[6] A memo was sent to French officers advising them of the United States' position, warning that Black people could "create for the white race in the Republic the menace of degeneracy."[7]

A Black woman in a Supreme Court justice's robe is another confounding symbol. At the White House in 2022, when Ketanji Brown Jackson accepted the nomination to the court, she said, "Among my many blessings—and indeed, the very first—is the fact that I was born in this great country. The United States of America is the greatest beacon of hope and democracy the world has ever known."[8] In her opening remarks at her confirmation hearing, she was unequivocal: "I hope that you will see how much I love our country and the Constitution, and the rights that make us free." She promised to "work productively to support and defend the Constitution and the grand experiment of American democracy that has endured over these past 246 years."[9] Her race and her country are not only compatible; they are complementary. One the means to improve the other.

The country has chosen to see things differently. Black veterans were largely excluded from the rights and privileges their service earned, such as educational benefits and home-buying assistance through the G.I. Bill. More than a few have been beaten or lynched while still in their uniforms. The year before Justice Jackson was confirmed, a uniformed army officer was returning home from weekend duty when he was erroneously pulled over by police, pepper-sprayed, yanked out of his car, and cuffed before being let go with no charges. As the officers prepared to release him, a warning was issued: they would end his career if he didn't "chill and let this go."[10] At Jackson's Supreme Court confirmation hearing, despite her multiple public declarations of love and respect for the country, she was accused of being an anti-American and antiwhite racist who took it easy on pedophiles.[11] It was bizarre.

How does it feel to be a problem? seems to stop its inquiry there. Being a problem feels like even when devoting your life to the country, skin color puts you, your commitment, or your place in the country up for question. Because your race and patriotism are deemed incompatible.

I see it differently. There is but one answer to the real question of how it feels to be a problem: Like power. It is agency.

In her 2018 book *Thick*, sociologist Tressie McMillan Cottom responds to a Black colleague's suggestion that *Black* was over, meaning the story has already been told. It'd been done, and new questions were needed. She writes, "The proclamation makes a mistake of assuming that Black people, like me, were only ever a problem and not a people."[12]

Problems can be solved; people cannot. Some have tried. It always results in disaster, in mass deaths. Black Americans are not problems to be solved, pieces to be puzzled together if they'd just fit in like they're supposed to. Du Bois says that the souls of Black folk neither want to "Africanize America" nor become white in America.[13] They simply want to share their unique message for a nation and a world. To be permitted to make the country wiser.

In an essay discussing *Native Son* a decade after it was published, the author Frantz Fanon writes, "In the end, Bigger Thomas acts. To put an end to his tension, he acts, he responds to the world's anticipation."[14] The future of Black America hinges on its ability to avoid that fate. And the future of the country cannot be uncoupled from its view of us—are we its people or its problem?

Whatever the answer, the American idea cannot be realized without us, and it cannot die without our permission. That is what it feels like to be a problem.

Genesis

Opinion Column, High School Newspaper
Raleigh, NC, March 1993
by M.D.

MINORITY VIEWPOINT:
ONE VOICE AMONG THE MASSES

It makes me feel good that in thirty minutes a small group of performers can raise so much power and emotion in a crowd. Yet the overall message of the Black History Month assembly seems somewhat hypocritical. The performers claim they want equality, but what they are doing is setting themselves and other ethnic, racial, and sexual groups apart.

To fully promote equality, all groups must be fully represented and open minded. This means the possibility of having a white history month as well as Asian, Indian,

Native American, etc., history month. I am not promoting racism or separation of ethnic groups; I am in fact, not even the slightest bit racist, but equality must be full equality, not just equality for one group of people. I was moved by the assembly, but it left me wondering what the future will hold.

The possible onset of reverse racism frightens me. All those years were spent fighting for equality and now it is beginning to happen again, except reversed. Blacks (I use the term only to describe my point) cannot and should not treat whites (again only for reference) as they feel their families were treated. This is unfair and unethical, two wrongs do not make a right. I admire Malcolm X and other civil right leaders; we would not be here today if not for them. I also think it is wonderful that their actions are celebrated, but we must celebrate the achievements of all persons that influenced our society. Heritage is very important to everyone, and heritage should be something to be shared. My point is that we should open our minds. Culture is extremely important; I believe that the African Tribal dances are the most powerful form of performing arts. I also enjoy the way they have influenced modern dance. The intermingling of culture and heritage is vital to society, not to mention stimulating.

"We will rise." "We shall overcome." These phrases scare me. I can't help but think that someone will. I believe that people should stand up for themselves and their heritage, but to have the goal of rising above all others is hypocritical.

Equality is just that, equality. There is no room to rise above another. Equality is here for everyone to appreciate, let's not let it slip away.

Together, as one large mass of brothers and sisters, we should fight to solve society's problems. There are starving babies and people living in cardboard boxes, the government is taking our money and destroying our planet. Let's combat these issues collectively, as one people, together for the same reasons, to better life for all. Peace and love to everyone.

• • •

Letter to the Editor, High School Newspaper
Raleigh, NC, April 1993
by Teddy Johnson III

Dear Editor,
In the March 1993 edition of *Sandscript*, I was overjoyed to read the effect of the Black History Month assembly on the audience. This "power and emotion," as stated in the article, "Minority Viewpoint: One Voice Among the Masses," unfortunately, was apparently raised in the wrong direction in the author.

The performers do want equality. Part of being equal includes being equal contributors to the society we live in. Fortunately, Black Americans have two things to contribute: our African heritage and culture, and our African American heritage and culture. These two things, though they sound alike, are quite different. Our African heritage stems from our ancestors who populated Western Africa. Our African American heritage is deeply rooted in the lifestyles of the people stolen from Africa and placed in this racist nation. In order to relate to people of other cultures, we must first be able to relate and have knowledge of our own. This point is vaguely recognized in the article in *Sandscript*; however, the statements following it eliminate its validity; I refer to the second paragraph in the article.

The writer claims that there should be a White, Asian, Indian, Native American, etc. history month as well. That's fine, but do not tell Black Americans this because it is not up to us to establish these months. These months must be established by the culture represented since these are the people that are hoping to spread a better understanding of their history and culture.

The writer was correct in saying, "equality must be full equality." I only wish someone had told this to Abraham Lincoln, the Supreme Court Justices presiding over the *Plessy vs. Ferguson* case, and other whites during those times who violated the Constitution. I wish someone would tell the city planners, judicial system officials, and groups who violate the Civil Rights Act of 1964 in these times.

The writer also mentioned that (for example only) Blacks should not treat whites as their forefathers were treated. A comparison between the treatment of Whites by Blacks now and the institution of slavery is not possible. The two situations are not equal in severity. Whites are no way in slavery, nor in danger of it. Two wrongs do not make a right, but it does make it even. Fortunately, the majority of the Black society is not seeking physical revenge. They are avenging slavery by excelling in a biased educational system and teaching other Blacks to use their mind for vengeance.

"We must celebrate the achievements of all persons." This is true, but why aren't the many black inventors, who invented everything from lawn mowers to spark plugs to gas masks, mentioned in history books?

The phrases "We will rise" and "We shall overcome" usually scare people who don't know what they mean. Fear is always present in the unknown. Blacks, in saying these phrases, do not want to rule the world, but only rise against the oppression that is put upon us by the world, and to be treated as equals.

"Together, as one large mass of brothers and sisters, we should fight to solve society's problems." I totally agree, but first we, all as Americans, must first acknowledge each other as brothers and sisters. "Peace and love to everyone."[1]

Acknowledgments

Bringing a book to life requires the time, resources, belief, and good fortune of many people and organizations. My deepest gratitude to the Emerson Collective fellowship and the democracy cohort for making this project possible. To my agent Gail Ross and my editor Patrik Henry Bass, thank you for seeing the vision, trusting me, and finding a way to make it all real. Michelle Lee, Carole Bell, Anne-Marie Slaughter, Rachel Thornton, Perry Bacon Jr., Tiffany Alexander, and Ahsante Bean, many thanks for reading and critiquing early essay drafts. Thank you to Erica Kim for sharing your story and Alex Cohen for sharing your talents. And to all the men and women I served with in locales around the world. To editors Jessica Lustig and Charles Homans of *The New York Times Magazine* and Theodore Kupfer, formerly of *National Review,* for the opportunity to write long-form articles for your audiences, essays that opened doors and appear herein. A debt of gratitude to David Shipley and

David Von Drehle of the *Washington Post* for the opportunity of a lifetime and for making me an infinitely better writer. To the countless scholars and colleagues whose work has influenced my learning, thinking, and understanding, I cannot thank you enough. This book is for all the family, friends, church members, and classmates, from Raleigh to Blakeley, who shaped my formative years. And most of all, to my wife and sons, siblings, and best friends, thank you for your love and patience.

Notes

CHAPTER I: AMERICAN HEATHEN

1. John Jay, "Federalist No. 2: Concerning Dangers from Foreign Force and Influence," *Independent Journal*, October 31, 1787.
2. "Declaration of Independence: A Transcription," US National Archives and Records Administration, last modified October 11, 2023, https://www.archives.gov/founding-docs/declaration -transcript.
3. Benjamin Franklin, "Constitutional Convention Address on Prayer" (speech delivered at the Constitutional Convention, Philadelphia, Pennsylvania, June 28, 1787).
4. George Washington to Jonathan Trumbull, July 20, 1788, in *The Writings of George Washington* (from the Original Manuscript Sources, 1745–1799. Edited by John C. Fitzpatrick. 39 volumes. Washington, DC: US Government Printing Office, 1931), 29:525.
5. Karen Armstrong, *A History of God: The 4,000-Year Quest of Judaism, Christianity and Islam* (New York: Ballantine Books, 1993), p. 3.

6. See Anthony Giddens, *Modernity and Self-Identity: Self and Society in the Late Modern Age* (Stanford, CA: Stanford University Press, 1991).

7. Jer. 29:11 (New International Version).

8. Rom. 8:28 (King James Version).

CHAPTER 2: DEMOCRACY WHEN BLACK, PARTS I & II

1. Astead W. Herndon, "Kamala Harris, Seeking a Campaign Jolt, Defends Record as Prosecutor," *New York Times*, June 9, 2019, https://www.nytimes.com/2019/06/09/us/politics/kamala-harris-2020-prosecutor-.html.

2. David Carlin, "Racial Prejudice in the 2008 Campaign," *Crisis*, September 29, 2008, https://www.catholicnewsagency.com/column/50457/racial-prejudice-in-the-2008-campaign.

3. "Limbaugh defends his Powell race comments," United Press International, October 20, 2008, https://www.upi.com/Top_News/2008/10/20/Limbaugh-defends-his-Powell-race-comments/17071224547602/.

4. "Rush: Colin Powell will vote for Obama again because melanin is thicker than water," *The Right Scoop*, August 29, 2011, https://therightscoop.com/rush-colin-powell-will-vote-for-obama-again-because-melanin-is-thicker-than-water/.

5. "Pat Buchanan: Black People Bought 'Propaganda' On The 'Liberal Plantation' (VIDEO)," *HuffPost*, September 30, 2011, https://www.huffpost.com/entry/pat-buchanan-black-liberal-plantation_n_988714.

6. See David A. Bositis, *Blacks & the 2012 Democratic National Convention* (Washington, DC: Joint Center for Political and

Economic Studies, 2012); and Ruth Igielnik, Scott Keeter, and Hannah Hartig, "Behind Biden's 2020 Victory," Pew Research Center, June 30, 2021, https://www.pewresearch.org/politics/2021/06/30/behind-bidens-2020-victory/.

7. Hannah Gilberstadt and Andrew Daniller, "Liberals make up the largest share of Democratic voters, but their growth has slowed in recent years," Pew Research Center, January 17, 2020, https://www.pewresearch.org/fact-tank/2020/01/17/liberals-make-up-largest-share-of-democratic-voters/.

8. "Political ideology among blacks by state," Pew Research Center, https://www.pewresearch.org/religion/religious-landscape-study/compare/political-ideology/by/state/among/racial-and-ethnic-composition/black/.

9. Louis Nelson, "Trump predicts he can win 95 percent of the black vote," *Politico*, August 19, 2016, https://www.politico.com/story/2016/08/donald-trump-african-american-vote-227218.

10. Molly Nagle and John Verhovek, "Biden faces backlash for comparing diversity in African American, Latino communities," ABC News, August 6, 2020, https://abcnews.go.com/Politics/biden-faces-backlash-comparing-diversity-african-american-latino/story?id=72218939.

11. Eric Bradner, Sarah Mucha, and Arlette Saenz, "Biden: 'If you have a problem figuring out whether you're for me or Trump, then you ain't black,'" CNN, May 22, 2020, https://www.cnn.com/2020/05/22/politics/biden-charlamagne-tha-god-you-aint-black/index.html.

12. J. R. Kerr-Ritchie, "Black Republicans in the Virginia Tobacco Fields, 1867–1870," *Journal of Negro History* 86, no. 1 (Winter 2001): pp. 12–29.

13. J. M. Kousser, *Colorblind Injustice: Minority Voting Rights and the Undoing of the Second Reconstruction* (Chapel Hill: University of North Carolina Press, 1999), p. 19.

14. Lee Formwalt, "Camilla Massacre," New Georgia Encyclopedia, last modified August 20, 2020, https://www.georgiaencyclopedia.org/articles/history-archaeology/camilla-massacre/.

15. "The Murder of Senator Benjamin Franklin Randolph," The History Engine, University of Richmond, https://historyengine.richmond.edu/episodes/view/5618, accessed February 17, 2024.

16. Michael F. Holt, *By One Vote: The Disputed Presidential Election of 1876* (Lawrence, KS: University Press of Kansas, 2008), p. 255.

17. See Keneshia N. Grant, *The Great Migration and the Democratic Party: Black Voters and the Realignment of American Politics in the 20th Century* (Philadelphia: Temple University Press, 2020).

18. Clark Clifford to Harry S. Truman, memorandum, November 19, 1947, https://www.trumanlibrary.gov/library/research-files/memo-clark-clifford-harry-s-truman.

19. "Dwight Eisenhower and the Central High Crisis," National Park Service, accessed February 17, 2024, https://www.nps.gov/people/dwight-eisenhower-and-the-central-high-crisis.htm.

20. Eric Schickler, "Lincoln's Party No More: The Transformation of the GOP," in *Racial Realignment: The Transformation of American Liberalism, 1932–1965* (Princeton: Princeton University Press, 2016), p. 258.

21. US Commission on Civil Rights, "Voting Rights and Political Representation in the Mississippi ," in Racial and Ethnic Tensions in American Communities: Poverty, Inequality, and Discrimination, Volume VII: The Mississippi Delta Report,

February 2001, https://www.usccr.gov/files/pubs/msdelta/ch3 .htm, accessed February 17, 2024.

22. Lilliana Mason, *Uncivil Agreement: How Politics Became Our Identity* (Chicago: University of Chicago Press, 2018), p. 6.

23. See Ismail K. White and Chryl Nicole Laird, *Steadfast Democrats: How Social Forces Shape Black Political Behavior* (Princeton: Princeton University Press, 2020).

24. Ashley Parker, Rachael Bade, and John Wagner, "Trump says they 'hate our country.' The Democrats he attacked say the country 'belongs to everyone,'" *Washington Post*, July 15, 2019, https://www.washingtonpost.com/politics/trump-calls-on -minority-congresswomen-to-apologize-after-he-said-they -should-go-back-to-their-countries/2019/07/15/897f1dd0-a6ef -11e9-a3a6-ab670962db05_story.html.

25. Nancy Pelosi (@SpeakerPelosi), https://twitter.com/Speaker Pelosi/status/1150408691713265665, accessed February 17, 2024.

26. John Lewis, "Speech at The March on Washington," August 28, 1963, https://voicesofdemocracy.umd.edu/lewis-speech-at-the -march-on-washington-speech-text/, accessed February 17, 2024.

27. Byron D'Andra Orey, "Black Legislative Politics in Mississippi," *Journal of Black Studies* 30, no. 6 (2000): pp. 791–814.

28. The evening telegraph. [volume] (Philadelphia [Pa.]), 31 Jan. 1870. Chronicling America: Historic American Newspapers. Lib. of Congress. https://chroniclingamerica.loc.gov/lccn/sn83 025925/1870–01–31/ed-1/seq-1/, accessed February 18, 2024.

29. New Era. "Mississippi Choice," (Washington, DC), Jan. 27 1870. https://www.loc.gov/item/sn84024437/1870–01–27/ed-1/, p. 2, accessed February 18, 2024.

30. Public Ledger. "Senator Revels–A Short History of Him," (Memphis, TN), Feb. 4 1870. https://www.loc.gov/item/sn850336 73/1870–02–04/ed-1/, p. 2, accessed February 18, 2024.

31. Terre Haute daily express. (Terre Haute, Ind.). January 25, 1870, https://newspapers.library.in.gov/?a=d&d=DWE18700125.1 .2&e=----en-20—1—txt-txIN----, accessed February 18, 2024.

32. Charlie Savage, "Incitement to Riot? What Trump Told Supporters Before Mob Stormed Capitol," *New York Times*, January 10, 2021, https://www.nytimes.com/2021/01/10/us/trump-speech-riot .html.

33. See "The Great Gallantry Of The Negro Troops At Milliken's Bend [Vicksburg Campaign]," *War of the Rebellion, Official Records of the Union and Confederate Armies*, Series III, vol. 3, pp. 452–53.

34. Tony Pettinato, "Reactions to First Black Senator in US History: Hiram Revels," GenealogyBank, February 25, 2020, https://blog.genealogybank.com/reactions-to-first-black-senator -in-us-history-hiram-revels.html, accessed February 18, 2024.

35. Timothy R. Smith, "Edward W. Brooke, First African American Popularly Elected to US Senate, Dies at 95," *Washington Post*, January 3, 2015, https://www.washingtonpost.com/politics /edward-w-brooke-first-african-american-elected-to-the-us-senate-dies-at-95/2015/01/03/cdabb80a-938b-11e4-ba53-a477d 66580ed_story.html, accessed February 18, 2024.

36. See Peter Beaumont, "Why Raphael Warnock Was Elected Georgia's First Black US Senator," *The Guardian*, January 6, 2021, https://www.theguardian.com/us-news/2021/jan/06/why -raphael-warnock-was-elected-georgia-first-black-us-senator; and Jeffrey Martin, "Loeffler Calls Warnock 'Most Radical

Candidate in America' as Georgia Senate Campaign Heats Up,"
Newsweek, November 13, 2020, https://www.newsweek.com
/loeffler-calls-warnock-most-radical-candidate-america-georgia
-senate-campaign-heats-1547108, accessed February 18, 2024.

37. See Sophie Lewis, "Raphael Warnock's Victory Speech Honors
Mother's '82-Year-Old Hands that Used to Pick Somebody Else's
Cotton'," CBS News, January 6, 2021, https://www.cbsnews.com
/news/raphael-warnock-victory-speech-mother-united-states
-senate-election-georgia-06–01–2021/, accessed February 18,
2024.

38. Tim Scott, Address at the 2020 Republican National
Convention, August 24, 2020, https://www.politico.com/video
/2020/08/24/tim-scott-our-family-went-from-cotton-to-congress
-in-one-lifetime-086109, accessed February 18, 2024.

39. Louis Nelson, "Sen. Tim Scott Reveals Incidents of Being
Targeted by Capitol Police," POLITICO, July 13, 2016, https://
www.politico.com/story/2016/07/tim-scott-capitol-racism-senate
-225507, accessed February 18, 2024.

40. Naina Bhardwaj , "Raphael Warnock's Dog Poop Advert Snaps
Back at Lofeller 'Smears' in Georgia Senate Runoff," *Business
Insider*, November 27, 2020, https://www.businessinsider.com
/raphael-warnocks-election-video-snaps-back-at-lofeller-2020-11,
accessed February 18, 2024.

41. Aaron Morrison, "Warnock Condemns Capitol Rioters in Post-
Election Sermon," *Associated Press*, January 10, 2021, https://
apnews.com/article/senate-elections-georgia-elections-riots-
jon-ossoff-8a603c46c220d2e3cd143d57a57a37ad, accessed
February 18, 2024.

42. Raphael Warnock, Sermon at Ebenezer Baptist Church, Atlanta, GA, January 24, 2021, https://www.youtube.com /watch?v=kbv9H2xNcDU&t=23s, accessed February 18, 2024.

CHAPTER 3: IS DEMOCRACY FOR WHITE PEOPLE?

1. Mary Hall, "US Presidents With the Largest Budget Deficits," Investopedia, September 28, 2023, https://www.investopedia.com /ask/answers/030515/which-united-states-presidents-have-run -largest-budget-deficits.asp.

2. Center for the Study of the American Constitution, "The Debate Over Religious Tests," https://csac.history.wisc.edu/document -collections/religion-and-the-ratification/religious-test-clause /religious-tests-and-oaths-in-state-constitutions-1776–1784/, accessed February 18, 2024.

3. See Donald Ratcliffe, "The right to vote and the rise of democracy, 1787—1828," *Journal of the Early Republic* 33, no. 2 (2013): pp. 219–254; and Richard R. John, "Affairs of office: the executive departments, the election of 1828, and the making of the democratic party" in *The Democratic Experiment: New Directions in American Political History* (Princeton: Princeton University Press, 2003): pp. 50–84.

4. Smith, Margaret Bayard, The First Forty Years of Washington Society (1906); Leish, Kenneth, (ed.) The American Heritage Pictorial History of the Presidents of the United States; Seale, William, The President's House vol. 1 (1986).

5. Sean Wilentz, "Politics, Irony, and the Rise of American Democracy," *Journal of the Historical Society* 6, no. 4 (2006): pp. 537–53.

6. See Timothy B. Tyson, "The Ghost of 1898: Wilmington Race Riot and the Rise of White Supremacy," *News & Observer*, November 17, 2016, https://media2.newsobserver.com/content/media/2010/5/3/ghostsof1898.pdf, accessed February 18, 2024.

7. Laura Mallonee, "The Nation's First Woman Senator Was a Virulent White Supremacist," *Smithsonian Magazine*, November 21, 2022, https://www.smithsonianmag.com/history/the-nations-first-woman-senator-was-a-virulent-white-supremacist-18098 1150/, accessed February 18, 2024.

8. Tyler Reny, "Why the GOP's Anti-Immigration Politics Are Here to Stay," *London School of Economics*, July 9, 2018, https://blogs.lse.ac.uk/usappblog/2018/07/09/why-the-gops-anti-immigration-politics-are-here-to-stay/, accessed February 18, 2024.

9. See the work of Julie Wronski, https://sites.google.com/site/juliewronski/research, accessed February 18, 2024.

CHAPTER 4: MODELING MINORITIES

1. Jacqueline Yi and Nathan R. Todd, "Internalized model minority myth among Asian Americans: Links to anti-Black attitudes and opposition to affirmative action," *Cultural Diversity and Ethnic Minority Psychology* 27 (2021): pp. 569–78, doi:10.1037/cdp0000448.

2. Ellen D. Wu, *The Color of Success: Asian Americans and the Origins of the Model Minority* (Princeton: Princeton University Press, 2014), pp. 6, 145–149.

3. Yi and Todd, "Internalized model minority myth," pp. 569–78.

4. Yi and Todd, pp. 569–78.

5. Yi and Todd, pp. 569–78.

6. Que-Lam Huynh, Thierry Devos, and Hannah R Altman, "Boundaries of American Identity: Relations between Ethnic Group Prototypicality and Policy Attitudes," *Political Psychology* 36 (2015): pp. 441–46, doi: 10.1111/pops.12189.

7. Roy F. Baumeister and Mark R. Leary, "The need to belong: Desire for interpersonal attachments as a fundamental human motivation," *Psychological Bulletin* 117 (1995): pp. 497–529, doi:10.1037/0033–2909.117.3.497.

8. Project Over Zero & American Immigration Council, "The Belonging Barometer: The State of Belonging in America," March 2023, https://www.projectoverzero.org/media-and-publications/belongingbarometer, accessed February 19, 2024.

9. William H. Frey, "Neighborhood segregation persists for Black, Latino or Hispanic, and Asian Americans," Brookings Institution, April 6, 2021, https://www.brookings.edu/articles/neighborhood-segregation-persists-for-black-latino-or-hispanic-and-asian-americans/.

10. Office of Communication and Community Relations, "TJHSST Offers Admission to 550 Students; Broadens Access to Students Who Have an Aptitude for STEM," Fairfax County Public Schools, June 23, 2021, https://www.fcps.edu/news/tjhsst-offers-admission-550-students-broadens-access-students-who-have-aptitude-stem.

11. Aaron Mak, "Why San Francisco's Asians Voted to Recall 'Progressive' Members of the School Board," *Slate*, February 17, 2022, https://slate.com/business/2022/02/san-francisco-school-board-recall-asian-americans.html.

12. Eric Ting, "San Francisco school board member Alison Collins used slur to describe Asian Americans in tweets," *SFGate*, March 21, 2021, https://www.sfgate.com/politics/article/Alison -Collins-San-Francisco-school-Asians-tweets-16038855.php.

13. Kimmy Yam, "Anti-Asian hate crimes increased 339 percent nationwide last year, report says," NBC News, February 14, 2022, https://www.nbcnews.com/news/asian-america/anti-asian -hate-crimes-increased-339-percent-nationwide-last-year-repo -rcna14282.

14. Kimmy Yam, "Viral images show people of color as anti-Asian perpetrators. That misses the big picture.," NBC News, June 15, 2021, https://www.nbcnews.com/news/asian-america/viral-images -show-people-color-anti-asian-perpetrators-misses-big-n1270821.

15. Neil Bennett, Donald Hays, and Briana Sullivan, "2019 Data Show Baby Boomers Nearly 9 Times Wealthier Than Millennials," United States Census Bureau, August 1, 2022, https://www.census .gov/library/stories/2022/08/wealth-inequality-by-household-type .html.

16. Rebecca Leppert, "A look at Black-owned businesses in the US," Pew Research Center, February 21, 2023, https://www .pewresearch.org/short-reads/2023/02/21/a-look-at-black-owned -businesses-in-the-u-s/.

CHAPTER 5: SOUND OF THE POLICE

1. 11Alive Staff, "Text: Atlanta mayor's speech to city during violent protests," 11Alive, May 30, 2020, https://www.11alive.com/article /news/local/atlanta-protests-mayor-speech-full-text/85–865bb 430–7502–44fa-a9b4–3414332ec342.

2. Martin Luther King Jr., "The Other America," April 4, 1967, https://www.crmvet.org/docs/otheram.htm.

3. Martin Luther King Jr., "The Other America," April 4, 1967.

4. Christopher Muller, "Northward Migration and the Rise of Racial Disparity in American Incarceration, 1880–1950," *The American Journal of Sociology* 118, no. 2 (2012): pp. 281–326.

5. YouGov, "Yahoo! News Race and Justice," May 31, 2020, https://docs.cdn.yougov.com/s23agrrx47/20200531_yahoo_race_and_justice_crosstabs.pdf, accessed February 18, 2024.

CHAPTER 6: SEMIQUIN

1. See Scott Bombay, "When Is the Real Independence Day: July 2 or July 4?," National Constitution Center, July 3, 203, https://constitutioncenter.org/blog/when-is-the-real-independence-day-july-2-or-july-4, accessed February 18, 2024.

2. Frederick Douglass, "Oration Delivered in Corinthian Hall, Rochester" (Rochester, NY: Lee, Man, and Co, 1852), pp. 14–37.

3. John Quincy Adams, Executive Order [on the deaths of Thomas Jefferson and John Adams] Online by Gerhard Peters and John T. Woolley, The American Presidency Project https://www.presidency.ucsb.edu/node/200526.

4. John Tyler, "An Address Delivered at the Celebration of the Fiftieth Anniversary of the Independence of the United States, in the Village of Ballston Spa," July 4, 1826.

5. Edward Everett, "An Oration Delivered at Cambridge, on the Fiftieth Anniversary of the Declaration of the Independence of the United States of America," July 4, 1826, https://books.google.com/books?id=ie4-AAAAYAAJ, accessed February 18, 2024.

6. Nathaniel S. Prime (Nathaniel Scudder), "The Year of Jubilee; but Not to Africans: A Discourse, Delivered July 4th, 1825, Being the 49th Anniversary of American Independence," Project Gutenberg, n.d., https://www.gutenberg.org/files/66487/66487-h/66487-h.htm, accessed February 18, 2024.

7. George Wyllys Benedict, "An oration, delivered at Burlington, Vt. on the fourth of July 1826: being the fiftieth anniversary of American independence" (Burlington, VT: E. & T. Mills, 1826), p. 22.

8. Joseph Penney, "A discourse delivered in the First Presbyterian Church in Rochester, on the morning of the Fourth of July, 1826" (Rochester, NY: Everard Peck, 1826), pp. 10–11.

9. Josiah Quincy, "An Oration Delivered on Tuesday, the Fourth of July, 1826, It Being the Fiftieth Anniversary of American Independence, Before the Supreme Executive of the Commonwealth and the City Council and Inhabitants of the City of Boston" (Boston: True and Greene, 1826), p. 23.

10. Adam Criblez, *Parading Patriotism: Independence Day Celebrations in the Urban Midwest, 1826–1876* (DeKalb, Illinois: Northern Illinois University Press, 2013), pp. 100–145.

11. "June 26, 1876: Proclamation Celebrating the Hundredth Anniversary of Independence," UVA Miller Center, https://millercenter.org/the-presidency/presidential-speeches/june-26-1876-proclamation-celebrating-hundredth-anniversary.

12. Criblez, *Parading Patriotism*, pp. 140–41.

13. Robert C. Winthrop, "Oration delivered before the City Council and citizens of Boston on the one hundredth anniversary of the Declaration of American Independence, July 4, 1876" (Boston: City Council, 1876), p. 85.

14. Susan B. Anthony, "Declaration of Rights of the Women of the United States - July 4, 1876" (speech delivered in Philadelphia, July 4, 1876).

15. Jake Noe, "'Everybody is Centennializing': White Southerners and the 1876 Centennial," *American Nineteenth Century History* 17, no. 3 (2016): pp. 325–43.

16. Criblez, *Parading Patriotism*, p. 141.

17. Noe, "'Everybody is Centennializing,'" p. 327.

18. George W. Williams, "The American Negro, From 1776 to 1876. Oration Delivered July 4, 1876, at Avondale, Ohio" (Cincinnati: Robert Clarke & Co., 1876), p. 28.

19. Williams, "The American Negro," p. 28.

20. Isaac T. Coates, "Centennial Fourth of July Oration, Delivered at Chester, Penna" (Philadelphia: J. B. Lippincott & Co., 1876), p. 56.

21. Ulysses S. Grant, "Gen. Grant's reasons for supporting Gen. Garfield. A sharply-drawn contrast. Speech at Warren, O., Sept. 28, 1880. . . . President Grant's letter in 1876 to Gov. Chamberlain, of South Carolina, on the Hamburg massacre [Washington, DC, 1880]," https://www.loc.gov/item/2020781915/.

22. Grant, "Gen. Grant's reasons for supporting Gen. Garfield."

23. Criblez, *Parading Patriotism*, p. 145.

24. "America's Greatest Flop," *Variety*, August 25, 1926, 1.

25. Calvin Coolidge, "Address at the Celebration of the 150th Anniversary of the Declaration of Independence in Philadelphia," The American Presidency Project, https://www.presidency.ucsb.edu/documents/address-the-celebration-the-150th-anniversary-the-declaration-independence-philadelphia.

26. Coolidge, "Address at the Celebration of the 150th Anniversary of the Declaration of Independence in Philadelphia."

27. "Official Plan for the Nation-Wide Celebration of the One Hundred and Fiftieth Anniversary of the Adoption of the Declaration of American Independence" (Washington, DC: Government Printing Office, 1926), p. 2.

28. "President Calvin Coolidge: Civil Rights Pioneer," Calvin Coolidge Presidential Foundation, last modified June 16, 2016, https://coolidgefoundation.org/blog/president-calvin-coolidge-civil-rights-pioneer/.

29. Lizabeth Cohen, "A consumers' republic: The politics of mass consumption in postwar America," *Journal of Consumer Research* 31 (2004): p. 239.

30. Langston Hughes, "I, Too" from *The Collected Works of Langston Hughes.*

31. *The Afro American,* July 3, 1926, https://news.google.com/newspapers?nid=UBnQDr5gPskC&dat=19260703&printsec=frontpage&hl=en, accessed February 18, 2024.

32. "Negro Exhibits at Sesqui," *The Monitor,* July 2, 1926, 1.

33. "Thousand Voices Impress Sesqui Crowd," *The Richmond Planet,* September 11, 1926, 8.

34. Gerald R. Ford, "Remarks at a Bicentennial Ceremony at the National Archives," The American Presidency Project, https://www.presidency.ucsb.edu/documents/remarks-bicentennial-ceremony-the-national-archives.

35. Gerald R. Ford, "Remarks at Naturalization Ceremonies at Monticello, Virginia," The American Presidency Project, https://www.presidency.ucsb.edu/documents/remarks-naturalization-ceremonies-monticello-virginia.

36. Ford, "Remarks at Naturalization Ceremonies at Monticello, Virginia."

37. Theodore M. Hesburgh, "Justice in America: The Dream and the Reality" (speech delivered at the National Citizens' Assembly on Improving Courts and Justice, Philadelphia, July 4, 1976).

38. "Rep. Barbara Jordan 1976 Democratic National Convention Keynote Speech Transcript," Rev, accessed July 12, 1976, https://www.rev.com/blog/transcripts/rep-barbara-jordan-1976 -democratic-national-convention-keynote-speech-transcript.

39. M. Todd Bennett, "The Spirits of '76: Diplomacy Commemorating the US Bicentennial in 1976," *Diplomatic History* 40 (2016): p. 706.

40. Hesburgh, "Justice in America."

CHAPTER 7: OUT OF MANY, TWONESS

1. James Baldwin, *Notes of a Native Son* (Boston: Beacon Press, 1955), p. 43.

2. W. E. B. (William Edward Burghardt) Du Bois, *The Souls of Black Folk* (Oxford: Oxford University Press, 2007), p. 2.

3. Du Bois, *Souls*, p. 3.

4. Joel Best and Gerald T. Horiuchi, "The Razor Blade in the Apple: The Social Construction of Urban Legends," *Social Problems* 32 (1985): 488–99, doi:10.2307/800777.

5. "The Buffalo Soldiers in WWI," National Park Service, accessed February 19, 2024, https://www.nps.gov/articles/the-buffalo -soldiers-in-wwi.htm.

6. W. E. B. Du Bois, "Documents of the War," *The Crisis*, May 1919, p. 16.

7. Du Bois, "Documents of the War," p. 16.

8. "Remarks by President Biden on his Nomination of Judge Ketanji Brown Jackson to Serve as Associate Justice of the US

Supreme Court," The White House, February 25, 2022, https://www.whitehouse.gov/briefing-room/speeches-remarks/2022/02/25/remarks-by-president-biden-on-his-nomination-of-judge-ketanji-brown-jackson-to-serve-as-associate-justice-of-the-u-s-supreme-court/.

9. Associated Press, "Read the full text of Supreme Court nominee Ketanji Brown Jackson's opening remarks," PBS, March 21, 2022, https://www.pbs.org/newshour/politics/read-the-full-text-of-supreme-court-nominee-ketanji-brown-jacksons-opening-remarks.

10. David K. Li and Tim Stelloh, "Virginia state authorities to investigate police who threatened Black Army officer," NBC News, April 10, 2021, https://www.nbcnews.com/news/us-news/police-accused-threatening-pulling-gun-black-army-lieutenant-during-virginia-n1263731.

11. Ed Pilkington, "Republicans turn Ketanji Brown Jackson hearing into a political circus," *The Guardian*, March 24, 2022, https://www.theguardian.com/us-news/2022/mar/24/ketanji-brown-jackson-republicans-senate-confirmation-hearing.

12. Tressie McMillan Cottom, *Thick: And Other Essays* (New York: The New Press, 2019), p. 132.

13. Du Bois, *Souls*, p. 4.

14. Frantz Fanon, *Black Skin, White Masks*, trans. Richard Philcox (New York: Grove Press, 2008), p. 139.

EPILOGUE: GENESIS

1. This is my first published piece, appearing in the high school newspaper two months before graduation, more than thirty

years ago. I don't recall why I was moved to write it, but the
op-ed pages of the *News & Observer*—the local paper—certainly
played a role. It fascinated me that there was an audience and
a market for sharing opinions about any and everything. And
there's so much to learn from other people's view of the world.
So when a classmate seemed puzzled and disenchanted in an
editorial about the school's Black History Month program—just
as I'd finished my first readings of *Native Son* and *The Souls of
Black Folks*—the moment seemed right to tell the school what
I thought in response. It was a time when I sported a high-top
fade, denim overalls with one strap hanging, and a leather
medallion with the African continent in red, black, and green
hanging around my neck. I felt as much a writer in Harlem in
the 1920s as in 1990s North Carolina with race-conscious
hip-hop entering mainstream.The morning the letter published,
a buzz built among the faculty. One of my teachers began class
with a discussion of it. Another congratulated me on a "fine
article" after class. The paper's faculty advisor caught me in the
hallway to tell me I had potential as a writer. My grandmother
was visiting the week it published, and I shared it with her and
my mother in the kitchen one evening. And they were effusive
in their praise. Maybe that was just because of mothers' love,
but I believed it. And after the military took me around the
world, generals and admirals took note of my writing, too, and
I finished my career speech writing for the nation's highest
ranking military officer. Two decades after this letter published,
I was preparing my exit from the military, publishing op-eds in
national publications about being Black in America.

Reading this now, I can see the same spirit here as has existed in nearly all my writing on race and America since. The nature of a writer is evident over broad sweeps of time. I take pride in the consistency of theme and approach. Little did I know—in fact, I could've never imagined in my wildest dreams—that the voice and ideas outlined in this letter would be the beginning of a life as a book author, scholar, and columnist for one of the nation's most prestigious newspapers. It's a dream come true.

It's also a reminder that there's value in sharing your opinion and view of things as a way to engage in constructive dialogue about our society and our future. A reminder that there is an audience and a market for essays from Black Americana, for essays that reveal a nation and its many peoples.

About the Author

THEODORE R. JOHNSON is a scholar on Black American electoral politics and a contributing columnist for the *Washington Post*. He is a retired commander in the United States Navy, serving for twenty years in a variety of positions, including as a White House Fellow, military professor, and speechwriter to the chairman of the Joint Chiefs of Staff. He is the author of 2021's *When the Stars Begin to Fall*, and his essays and opinion pieces have appeared in a variety of publications and featured on all the major cable news outlets. He has taught graduate students at Northeastern University, Georgetown University, and the University of Southern California. Ted is a proud member of the Omega Psi Phi Fraternity, Inc., and an HBCU graduate holding degrees from Hampton University, Harvard University, and Northeastern University.